MW01087291

LITTLE RUSSIAN PHILOKALIA

SERIES

LITTLE RUSSIAN PHILOKALIA
V
ST. THEODORE OF SANAXAR

Icon of St. Theodore of Sanaxar, painted for his glorification in 1999.

Troparion to St. Theodore of Sanaxar
Tone 4
From thy youth thou didst love Christ with filial love, *
and desiring only to serve the Lord * thou didst choose the
good part, which shall not be snatched away by death. * Thou
didst devote thyself to the one thing needful and to the Giver of
Life, * and from Him thou wast vouchsafed the gifts of Divine
teaching and spiritual discernment, * guiding all having recourse
to thee and seeking salvation of soul, * O Divinely wise Elder
Theodore of Sanaxar.

LITTLE RUSSIAN
PHILOKALIA

VOLUME V

Saint Theodore of Sanaxar

Translated by the St. Herman of Alaska Brotherhood

ST. HERMAN OF ALASKA BROTHERHOOD

2000

Address all correspondence to:
St. Herman of Alaska Brotherhood
P. O. Box 70
Platina, California 96076

FIRST EDITION

Front cover: Engraving from the first edition (1847) of the *Life of Elder Theodore,* by S. Miloskovsky.
Back cover: Carved icon of St. Theodore from Sanaxar Monastery.

Photographs not otherwise credited were provided by the monks of the Sanaxar Monastery.

Library of Congress Cataloging in Publication Data

Theodore of Sanaxar, St. (1719–1791)
Little Russian Philokalia, Vol. V: St. Theodore of Sanaxar
    Translated from the Russian.

Library of Congress Catalogue Card Number: 00-104364
ISBN: 0-938635-34-4

CONTENTS

INTRODUCTION

A CLOSE FRIEND'S DEATH shattered his world. Shaken to the core he began to lament the wayward life he had been leading. As he turned in his grief to God, a spark of purpose flashed in his soul. He became instantaneously transformed. He refused to look back at his once outwardly promising career and boldly set out for the isolated wilderness, desiring to dedicate his life to God as best he knew.

The young Theodore's thirst for his new life of desert-dwelling was an expression of new, raw energy welling up within him. At that time this thirst was one-sided, for he had no one to teach him, no spiritual father, no guide. The townspeople in the place where he settled, careful not to taint themselves through contact with some vagrant, not only did not give him a piece of bread, but beat him mercilessly and drove him away.

But the fire within him could not be so easily quenched. He courageously continued on, striving to take the Kingdom of Heaven by violence (cf. Matt. 11:12) without showing any pity to himself. He took refuge in a monastery. He learned to fear God and no one else. The Holy Fathers became his instructors on his lonely path. In time, as he matured, he learned to observe the proper measure at each step, advancing in faith, in purity and knowledge of his sinfulness before God.

Becoming a spiritual guide in his own right, young men and women flocked to him, seeking with stubborn determination to become citizens of Heaven even in this present life. This compelled him to find the right answers for others; and through prayer and enlightenment from the Holy Spirit, he drew on the wisdom, life and practice of the Church of Christ, and by the grace of God his soul was informed how to direct them.

Later, into one such disciple, the future St. Herman of Alaska, did Elder Theodore breathe his desert-loving vision. It was St. Herman who was later, after the death of Elder Theodore, to bring the light of Christ's Gospel to the shores of North America. He, in turn, would make his own life the model for spiritual ascent to God in the New World. The events of St. Herman's life clearly mirror those of his great teacher Elder Theodore: his love of solitude, homeless wandering, enduring privations and open persecution from the authorities, the protection of the oppressed, intercession before authorities, and guidance of others along the path to God.

On the Feast of Pentecost in 1991 Elder Theodore's monastery was re-opened. The monastery suffered great spiritual trials in 1994-1995, but has now emerged with great vigor as one of the great spiritual centers of Russia today. The brotherhood, which currently numbers eighty monks and novices, is spiritually guided by Schema-Archimandrite Pitirim and Schema-Abbot Jerome in the tradition of the newly glorified St. Theodore of Sanaxar.

May the appearance in the English language of the life and teaching of St. Theodore of Sanaxar spur all who love God to forge courageously ahead and become partakers of the mystical banquet of our Lord Jesus Christ. Amen!

Hieromonk Gerasim

Chronology

1719   Birth of Elder Theodore.
1739   Desert dweller near White Sea.
1748   August 14. Tonsured a monk.
1757   Transfer to Sarov Monastery.
1759   Transfer to Sanaxar Monastery.
1762   December 13. Ordained to the priesthood.
1764   October 16. Elevated as Abbot of the Monastery.
1767   Construction of main church begins.
1774   Exiled to Solovki.
1783   Released from Solovki.
1788   Repose of Hieromonk Benedict, Superior of Sanaxar
      Monastery.
1791   February 19. Repose of Elder Theodore.
1991   Pentecost. Sanaxar Monastery reopened.
1999   April 21. Uncovering of the holy relics of St. Theodore.
1999   June 28. Glorification of St. Theodore.

Main church of Sanaxar Monastery, dedicated to the Nativity
of the Theotokos. Photo from winter of 1998.

I

The Life of Elder Theodore, Abbot of the Sanaxar Monastery

A desert dweller's cell in the Russian North. Line drawing by E. Soboleva.

THE LIFE OF

Elder Theodore

ABBOT OF THE SANAXAR MONASTERY

who is commemorated on the 19th of February (†1791)

The following biography of Elder Theodore is primarily based on the 1847 edition of his Life* and was written through the collaboration of the Sarov Abbot Isaac Putilov, the brother of Elders Moses and Anthony of Optina, evidently in conjuction with their life in the Roslavl forests where those desert dwellers were scrupulously collecting and copying such soul-profiting texts. This Life therefore comes from the very heart of Russian desert-lovers. It is augmented with recent editions, which add biographical dates from other sources.

1. ALONE AGAINST THE WORLD

WITHIN the confines of the Yaroslavl Province, near the town of Roma-nov by the River Volga, a prince by the name of Ignatius Ushakov lived with his wife Parasceva [according to some sources, Irene]. A son, who in holy Baptism was named John, was born to them in the year 1719. When he came of age he was enlisted in the Preobrazhensky Guard Regiment in the Im-perial Capital, Petersburg, where he was soon promoted to the rank of ser-geant and continued his duty.

---

* *The Life of Fr. Theodore, Former Abbot of Sanaxar Monastery, Who Reposed in 1791 on the 19th of February* (Moscow, University Press, 1847). The Life was dedicated to the Sanaxar Monastery by the editors at Optina Monastery near Kozelsk.

Life in such a famous city, in the circle of his peers and amid the usual merriments, was not without harm to his soul—*evil communications corrupt good manners* (I Cor. 15:33). But our God Who loves mankind, not wishing the death of the sinner, but that he would turn to Him and live (cf. Ez. 33:11), by His special Providence arranged that this young John would turn away from the path of licentiousness in the following way.

When he was once making merry with his comrades, one of them suddenly fell to the ground and died. This produced great terror and lamentation in all of them, but it was John most of all who was moved in soul. Casting everything aside, he then resolved to flee into the wilderness, according to the words of the Prophet David, *Lo, I have fled afar off and have dwelt in the wilderness, I have waited upon God Who saveth me* (Ps. 54:7–8).*

He ordered his valet to prepare his horses and everything necessary for the road, with the stated intention of travelling to his father's house. Leaving Petersburg in this way and having travelled several miles beyond it, he dismissed his servant to return together with the horses and everything needed for the journey, while he continued alone with the intention of finding a place for himself in the wooded coastlands. Walking along the road near the city of Yaroslavl in the guise of a poor laborer, he met his uncle and servants but, due to his poor apparel, was not recognized. Seeing his uncle, he was greatly troubled in soul, recalling to mind his former way of life which he had spent in abundance and ease. However, the fire of Divine love burning in his heart vanquished the thought and unwaveringly beckoned him to dwell in the wilderness.

After a time he came to the regions along the northern Dvina and, walking through the forests near the White Sea, he found in a certain spot an abandoned cell. There he began to live in solitude worshipping God alone. He was then twenty years old. He spent three years in this place, suffering great affliction and starvation. The nearby inhabitants brought him only the

---

*A similar incident is recorded in the Life of Blessed Xenia of Petersburg, a contemporary of Elder Theodore. Her husband fell down and died at a drinking party and this so shook her soul that she took up a life of repentance to pray for the salvation of her husband who had died without repentance. The possibility exists that her husband, Andrew Fyodorovich, was also the close friend of Elder Theodore.

most necessary food, which barely enabled him to escape death from hunger. Since the surrounding inhabitants had been enjoined not to allow desert-dwellers to live in their forest,* at those times when he would come to the village for his needs, the inhabitants would subject him to indescribable beatings, wounding him with heavy blows. They would drive him away to the city of Archangelsk in such a state that only by the most fervent entreaties was he barely able to escape with his life.

Due to such straitened circumstances he was forced to leave that region and move south to the lands of Kiev. Having reached the coenobitic Ploschansk Monastery, he asked the Abbot of this monastery with the utmost humility to accept him into the monastery, stating that he was the son of a clergyman.** For a long time the Abbot would not accept him due to his lack of identification, but acceding to his heart-stricken request the Abbot finally accepted him and assigned him to fulfill the obedience of psalm reader. As he was reading, the Abbot observed that he did not seem to be from the family of a clergyman, but rather from nobility or the family of some ruler. Fearing that some sort of repercussions might take place in the monastery from a violation of civil ordinances, if it were to be discovered that he was some noble or a landowner's son, he ordered him to live near the monastery in the forest. Cells were to be found there which had been built by previous desert-dwellers who had lived there praying to God. He settled in those cells, having received a blessing from these fathers.

2. MONASTIC LIFE IN THE CAPITAL

Soon, in conformity with Imperial decrees, an investigating team was sent to destroy such dwellings and to arrest those living in them. John, who did not have documents, was caught. Since he revealed in the presence of the interrogators that he was a sergeant of the Guard who had secretly fled, he

---

*Government authorities had issued such regulations to control the populace and monitor sectarian movements.

** Monastic life had begun to be regulated by decrees of Peter the Great at the beginning of the eighteenth century and an officer of the Guard would have encountered legal obstacles to the monastic life.

was taken to Empress Elizabeth Petrovna of blessed memory. He was led into the courtyard, and while a report was being compiled, they stationed him beneath the Royal porch.

Hearing of him, many of the guards came to the palace expressly to have a look at him. The sight was enough to evoke genuine contrition. From his great abstinence, he was withered. His face was pale, and he was dressed in a hair shirt girded at the waist. When he was led in before the Empress at her demand, she asked him, "Why did you desert my regiment?"

He replied, "For my soul's salvation, Your Majesty."

She responded, "I forgive your flight and restore you to your rank."

At this John said, "I, in devoting myself to God and the salvation of my soul, wish to persevere to the end, Your Majesty. I do not desire my former life and rank."

The Empress said unto him: "Why did you leave secretly? Having had a desire for such a good work, could you not have been given a discharge by us?"

To this John replied, "If I had bothered Your Majesty about myself, you would not have believed that I, a young man, could have borne such a yoke. Now I have been tested in the spiritual life and I wish to trouble Your Majesty to bless me to continue in it until death."

The Empress said, "Let it be so. I permit you to enter this calling, only you must remain here in the St. Alexander Nevsky Lavra."

John obeyed the Monarch's will and desire. Soon, by her express decree, he was tonsured (at 29 years of age) in the presence of the Empress herself on the 13th of August in 1748. At the order of Archbishop Theodosius who then governed the monastery, he was named Theodore in tonsure, in honor of the Right-believing Grand Prince Theodore, the Wonderworker of Yaroslavl, who is commemorated on September 19.

Thus, the newly tonsured monk Theodore began to reside permanently in that monastery, paying heed to his salvation, exerting himself in fasting and prayer, and loving stillness. When God wanted to test His slave, He allowed him first to experience warfare of the flesh. Theodore was himself puzzled as to where it came from. By unceasing prayer he petitioned the Lord, asking deliverance from this passion, and increased his fasting for a long time,

Empress Elizabeth Petrovna.

even to the point of exhausting his flesh. Seeing His slave in such conflict, God had mercy on him and lightened his warfare.

Soon, however, from the envy of the adversary, a different, outer warfare commenced. Knowing Theodore's truly good, ascetic life, Empress Elizabeth Petrovna regarded him with favor, and whenever she happened to be in that monastery she always asked whether or not he had suffered injury from anyone. He would reply that he hadn't borne any insult from anyone. Emperor Peter Fyodorovich, being at that time the heir, would often state that in the St. Alexander Nevsky Monastery there was an unusual monk, Ushakov. He revered his piety, his ascetic and distinct appearance, his humble and virtuous life. Many Petersburg citizens who wished to live a God-pleasing life in the world began to come to him—men, together with women and children. Fervently they would request his instruction as to how they, living in the world, could please God. He declined to do this, noting the presence of many learned men in the monastery who could sufficiently and quite happily instruct others. Their faith, however, finally persuaded him to begin to instruct them.

Finding himself incapable of giving the right solution to every demand of the lay folk, and unable to sufficiently satisfy their spiritual needs, he began unceasingly to entreat the Lord God. He besought God, if it were His Divine will, to enlighten his mind to understand the Scriptures; that thereby, through his unworthiness, he would be able to give instructions and solutions to the unfortunate ones who came to him. Then the thought came to him to read the Homilies of St. John Chrysostom and he learned much from reading them. The number of people who turned to him for spiritual profit, and for the resolution of their difficulties from the Scriptures, kept increasing more and more.

Seeing that people were coming to the simple Elder for instruction, the learned monks who lived in the monastery considered this to be an insult and contempt on the Elder's part, and informed His Eminence Sylvester (who had succeeded Archbishop Theodosius) that a simple monk, attracting people to himself, was creating a disturbance and scandal in the monastery. Hearing sufficient reports, and seeing this for himself, the bishop ordered the Steward to forbid entrance into the monastery to those who said that they

Holy Trinity Cathedral at St. Alexander Nevsky Lavra.

had come to see the monk Theodore. This caused great sorrow for those who had been coming to him in earnest and who were joined to him with spiritual love.

Fr. Theodore, seeing this unrighteous decree, came to the Steward's cell and with his habitual modesty said to him, "I ask your reverence to explain to me for what cause you have forbidden entrance into the monastery to those who wish to come to me for spiritual benefit?" The Steward replied, "So that you might not presume to undertake the task of instructing others, and so that you don't attract crowds of people to yourself and thereby disturb the monastery." Fr. Theodore said, "If something in my teaching seems unlawful to His Eminence, then let him question me, but to bring sorrow without cause on those who desire spiritual profit is sinful." These words were reported to His Eminence. Although the bishop was wroth, he nevertheless ordered that people who wished to see Fr. Theodore be admitted.

Nevertheless, certain of the brethren did not afterwards cease grieving Fr. Theodore; yet he did not despond. Placing his hope in everything on God's will, without which, according to the words of the Gospel, *not a hair of your head shall perish* (Luke 21:18), he continued to instruct, heal, comfort and strengthen everyone who came to him, thus heeding the saying of Sirach, *Better a word than a gift [alms]* (Sirach 18:16). Likewise, St. John Chrysostom, in his 25th Moral Discourse on the Acts of the Apostles, says: "You can [give alms] with counsel and this is much greater than all; this is better than all—much greater than possessions. For in so doing you put away not starvation, but a grievous death."* Again, in Homily 46, part II, on the Book of Genesis, he says: "It often happens that a pleasant word is greater to a pauper than alms." And the Holy Apostle Paul who teaches: *If any provide not for his own, ... he hath denied the faith and is worse than an infidel* (I Tim. 5:8). And as those who earnestly came to Fr. Theodore—in their afflictions of soul, in perplexities and in despair—received from him instruction and healing, they were so bound to him by Godly love that they entrusted their entire lives to him along with that of their wives and children. Whatever he might tell them, with joy did they take pains to fulfill with all diligence.

Among themselves his disciples were like brothers from the same womb and—even better—there was not to be found among them either envy, deceit, strife, or jealousy. Rather, they maintained a marvelous harmony and oneness of soul with meekness and humility. They were all given instructions by Fr. Theodore to guard against all of the sinful passions which war against the soul (cf. I Peter 2:11), since whoever is a friend of the world becomes an enemy to God (cf. James 4:4); to endure for the love of God all afflictions with thanksgiving and joy for, according to the word of Christ, in the world sorrow is inevitable, but our sorrows shall be turned to joy (cf. John 16:20). *Your heart shall rejoice and your joy no man taketh from you* (John 16:22). They were to be moderate in food and drink, to eat for sustenance and not to

---

*Homilies on the Acts of the Apostles," in *Nicene and Post-Nicene Fathers,* Volume XI (Grand Rapids: Eerdmans Publishing Co., 1980), p. 166.

excess, to wear clothing neither too tattered nor luxurious. On feast days Fr. Theodore instituted the following practice: one of his more adroit disciples, able to read the books of the Sacred Scriptures or of the Holy Fathers with commentary, would do so while the others would come to hear the reading. Those who had specific spiritual needs would come to the monastery, to Fr. Theodore to resolve their problems. Fr. Theodore also gave them a prayer rule. In every sense, their way of life was soul-saving.

But the adversary who hates what is good did not cease to plague Fr. Theodore's disciples with his snares by means of depraved people. They called them sanctimonious and sometimes schismatics, but all of this was endured with joy for the sake of God's love. Annoyance from those who wished ill towards Fr. Theodore increased because of the fact that people came to him for instruction. It came also from others since, when he was given the obedience to stand on guard beside the relics of St. Alexander Nevsky, he began to deposit into the monastery treasury a larger amount than other hieromonks had done who had previously had the same obedience. Such envious people would have gone so far as to have him sent to some distant monastery. But, since he had been assigned there by Imperial decree, without Her Majesty's order nothing could be done against him. Fr. Theodore could have informed Empress Elizabeth herself about all of the malice which was being heaped upon him, but he said nothing concerning his own lot and endured everything nobly.

3. SAROV MONASTERY

Having thus endured for ten years, he judged it right to give place to anger, according to Christ's words: *When they persecute you in this city, flee ye into another* (Matt. 10:23), and he decided to move from the St. Alexander Nevsky Monastery to Sarov Monastery, which he had previously wished to enter. Hearing of his desire, those with enmity against him ordered him to submit a written request. Having received this, they quickly negotiated his release. Thus it was that in 1757* he headed on his way rejoicing, taking with him those disciples of his, bound to him by spiritual love, both men and

---

*This was about the same year that St. Herman of Alaska was born.

View of Sarov Monastery from the north. Drawing by E. Soboleva.

women, who had secured their release from the regional authorities. Going from the west to the east, they followed in the steps of their father. Having arrived in Arzamas, the Elder settled the women—at the time a small number—who were wandering with him for the sake of God's love, in the Arzamas St. Nicholas Convent. Meanwhile, he travelled on with his male disciples and entered the Sarov Monastery.

A short time later his women disciples moved from the St. Nicholas Monastery in Arzamas to the vacant Alexeyevsky Convent where, by God's grace and by the prayers of their kind instructor, this community soon grew to fifty sisters and more. Everything in their life was regulated by a special rule: food and drink, clothing, prayer, vigil, handiwork, and their interaction, which will be spoken of later.

Having lived two years in Sarov Monastery, Fr. Theodore—because of the fact that the number of his disciples had significantly increased—asked the Abbot, Elder Ephraim, and the senior fathers of Sarov to place at his disposal the impoverished Sanaxar monastery. Situated twenty-five miles away near the city of Temnikov on the Moksha River, it was at that time under the auspices of Sarov Monastery. In 1759, when his request had been fulfilled, he immediately moved to the Sanaxar Monastery with all of his disciples where they began to struggle in every praiseworthy endeavour.

Sanaxar Monastery had first been established in 1659, during the reign

View of St. Nicholas Arzamas Convent in the nineteenth century.

Abbot Ephraim of Sarov.

of Tsar Alexei Mikhailovich—with the blessing of the Patriarch of Moscow, at the initiative of the Temnikov recorder Luke Evsyukov; and by the citizens of the city of Temnikov and other surrounding villages. Evsyukov invited Abbot Theodosius from the Old Kadom Monastery, about forty miles from Sanaxar, and he became the first Abbot. In 1676, with the blessing of the Patriarch of Moscow Ioasaph II, the first church was built in the monastery in honor of the Meeting of the Vladimir Icon of the Theotokos. The monastery received its name from the small lake Sanaxar that is situated below its walls, for in the local dialect it literally means that "it lies on an elevated spot in a swampy gully." After its closure and liquidation in the eighteenth century it was administered by Sarov Monastery.*

Since its main structures and the holdings which belonged to it—summer houses, forest stands, hay fields and fishing grounds—were in various hands, this caring father started out in the monastery with plenty of difficulty. Nonetheless, he petitioned for the return of these properties and secured them once again for the monastery. After moving from Sarov to the Sanaxar Monastery, in which there was one small wooden church and several wooden cells, they began at first to build wooden cells with storerooms. Those who wished to save their souls began to gather together in this hermitage, first from Petersburg, then from Moscow, where an epidemic was raging. The brethren, meanwhile, began to increase with every passing hour.

His Eminence Pachomius, Bishop of Tambov, then the diocesan bishop, and knowing Fr. Theodore, summoned him and persuaded him to become the Superior. In addition, he persuaded him to accept ordination to the priesthood, although Fr. Theodore had declined this many times. Being elevated by the hierarch to the priesthood on December 13, 1762, he returned to the monastery and began to serve the Lord God in the celebration of the Liturgy with a pure conscience. When he served Liturgy there could be seen on him a sign worthy of amazement—his face shone with a certain unusual pale rosy-pink light, circular in form, on both of his cheeks. Thus was the Divine Scripture fulfilled in him: *A glad heart maketh a cheerful countenance* (Prov. 15:13).

---

*It had been closed by Imperial decree of Peter the First during the first half of the eighteenth century.

4. SANAXAR MONASTERY ORDER

The following rule was laid down in the monastery. The Divine service and reading in the holy church was not to be hasty, so that it could be comprehensible even to the simplest people. For this reason, the church services would last an hour and a half at Vespers on weekdays, an hour at Compline, five hours at Matins, and two hours and more for Liturgy. But, for the most part on weekdays—to alleviate the burden upon the small number of priests—the Hours were served in place of Liturgy, and would last up to an hour and a half. In all, during the twenty-four hours in the day, the services would last nine hours, while on Sundays and on days with a *polyeleos* service, ten or more. When a Vigil would occur, the services would last twelve hours within that twenty-four-hour period.

From such unhurried reading, those present experienced the special power of the awakening of the soul, everyone speaking to themselves in psalms, and hymns and spiritual songs, singing and making melody in their hearts to the Lord (cf. Eph. 5:19). Fr. Theodore's reasoning for this unhurried reading was that, "When we read quickly, we fill the air without understanding the power of the Scriptures. Then, how can the soul come to sense anything, according to the word of the holy Apostle Paul—if in warfare *the trumpet gives an uncertain sound, who shall prepare himself to the battle?* (I Cor. 14:8). Not the reading of the Scriptures but its power understood by us will be unto salvation. The holy Prophet David spoke concerning this, that *the unfolding of Thy words will give light and understanding unto babes* (Ps. 118:130), that is, to beginners—as babes according to the spirit—who do not know the higher stages of prayer."

The following cell rule of prayer was given: after coming from Matins everyone must read the morning prayers and the general commemoration; and in the evening, after the dismissal from church at Compline, the Jesus Prayer 300 times, and with this 150 prostrations in decades (that is, ten prayers by themselves and ten with prostrations). But, in church, other than the Canon to the Theotokos according to the eight tones from the *Theotokarion*, no other canons were read. With regard to prostrations, the usual ecclesiastical order was followed, regulating when prostrations were to be made in church, and whether they were to be full prostrations or bows. The same were to be made in the cells.

Upon leaving the cell for church, as well as leaving the church for one's cell, the following prayers were read, with prostrations: *O God, be merciful unto me a sinner,* and a prostration; *O God, cleanse my sins and have mercy on me,* and a prostration; *Without measure have I sinned, O Lord, forgive me,* and a prostration; *Before Thy Cross, we bow down, O Master, and Thy Holy Resurrection, we glorify,* and a prostration; then *It is truly meet...* and a prostration; *Glory...,* *both now...,* *Lord, have mercy,* three times, *Bless, O Lord,* and the usual dismissal—if one is not a priest, then this dismissal: *O Lord Jesus Christ, Son of God, through the prayers of Thy Most Pure Mother, through the intercessions of my Guardian Angel and the other heavenly bodiless hosts, the honorable and glorious Prophet, Forerunner and Baptist John, the holy, glorious and all-praised Apostles, the holy, glorious and right-victorious Martyrs, our Venerable and God-bearing Fathers and of Saint* _____ [who is commemorated on that day], *and of all Thy saints, have mercy and save me, a sinner,* and then three prostrations.

After entering the church every brother, standing in his assigned place and with the fear of God, would begin the appointed prayers with prostrations, bowing to the brothers on both sides as is customary. Everyone was to stand in his own place with reverence, not only without saying anything to anyone, but not even looking at anyone without need. Likewise, it was to be observed that prostrations were not to be made just at any time, but so that everyone followed the reader or chanter and would bow together during the reading of *Alleluia...,* *Holy God...,* and *O come let us worship....* In general, *all things* among them were *done decently and in order,* according to the word of the Holy Apostle Paul (cf. I Cor. 14:40).

Concerning food it was observed that following the meal in the refectory, no one would take anything to his cell except kvass. Only one or two books for spiritual benefit would be issued. Concerning latches and locks for the cells, as well as concerning wine and baths, it was a shame even to speak of them. The food consisted of only that which was most necessary, that is, only that which was impossible to dispense with. Hence, pies and other white bread items were not served—not even on the Bright Resurrection of

Christ—unless they had been sent by someone. It was not permitted for anyone to have a fire in his cell except for those performing handicrafts. The cells were heated only when necessary and, having warmed the cell, the fire was again put out. Common obediences, such as fishing and hay gathering, were shared by all the brothers—both the church servers and those who were occupied with handicrafts (except the infirm and aged). Leaving their crafts, all would go out together, and the father and caring shepherd of their souls would go with them.

5. THE SPIRITUAL PHYSICIAN

According to the words of the monastery chronicle, Fr. Theodore, "possessing this sacred rank of the priesthood, in his governance of this monastery and all the brethren therein, worthily fulfilled the responsibilities of Superior. He taught the true faith and piety to everyone who came to him or who desired to lead a God-pleasing life; for as he had led an exemplary monastic life in piety for many years, he was adorned with excellent gifts. He had exceptional skill in teaching, and his discernment was penetrating and extensive. He also had other superb qualities in matters concerning ordinary human affairs. He was by no means inclined to the acquisition of the glory and wealth of this world, but loved most of all seclusion and meditation on the divine words. He devoted his life to labors and to caring for the salvation of men's souls."*

The most salvific thing that was instituted by our Father in this monastery was the following: whenever thoughts contrary to salvation would arise in a brother, he was obliged to go that very hour to the Abbot, no matter what time it was, even if it was during the night. And he, as their child-loving father, and caring for their salvation, received each one in a fatherly way and healed the soul wounded by the enemy. He would spend an hour or two, or sometimes more with such a one, and would not dismiss him from his cell until he had restored that soul to perfect health. Those brothers would say themselves that after leaving his cell, they felt such enlightenment in their conscience, that they had forgotten every earthly thought.

---

* *Life of Our Holy Father St. Theodore of Sanaxar* (Sanaxar Monastery, 1999), pp. 25–26.

What grace of God in the Elder's word soothed their souls! Hence many of his disciples reckoned themselves blessed to have found themselves in obedience to such a father.

The Elder frequently gave instruction, sometimes in the refectory and sometimes in his cell—on how one must live in the monastery, how to cut off one's will, how to walk the narrow and sorrowful path of the monastic life and not to turn back, and how to seek a spiritual father according to the teaching of St. Basil the Great, as set forth in the *Prologue* for the 7th of March. Concerning this, St. John of the Ladder explains that the entire endeavor of the monastic life consists in cutting off one's will and understanding, and in the forsaking of one's kin and riches. Without this, one living in a monastery is not a monk, but only a worldly person. How is it possible for a ship to sail without a pilot, to learn some kind of art without material and a teacher? And it is even more impossible for one entering the monastic life without an experienced guide to save one's soul, which the holy Climacus terms the "art of arts" (cf. Step 4:73).

But his disciples would ask him, "Father, if someone is unable to find a father to whom he might entrust his body and soul, what can you say about this?" He told them this: "Listen, my friends, to what the Son of God says, *He who seeks shall find* (Matt. 7:8). Whoever truly desires the monastic life must only seek a father, and the Lord God will not abandon him in this and will undoubtedly help him to find one. To trust oneself is extremely dangerous, as it is said, *lest ye be wise in your own conceits* (Rom. 11:25). Hence, in case of need, if one entrusts himself in the Lord to a worthy brother, he does well. If by this, according to the Lord's word, he walks the narrow path, then the Lord God will secretly instruct him unto salvation."

6. THE GROWTH OF THE COMMUNITY

In the meantime the number of brethren in the Sanaxar Monastery increased steadily. However, as they had still not been tonsured into the monastic habit, it was necessary to obtain permission for the tonsure.* When the

---

*The ecclesiastical reforms of Peter the First regulated how many monks could live in a specific monastery.

Sovereign Empress Catherine II was informed of this through Count Alexis Gregorievich Orlov, by an Imperial decree of April 23, 1763, she ordered that all of Fr. Theodore's brothers be tonsured. "In 1764 Empress Catherine II issued a decree regulating the number of monasteries. The rest were to be closed. The Sanaxar Hermitage was numbered among those to be liquidated, but it remained open through the mediation of Fr. Theodore. By a decree of October 16, 1764, Fr. Theodore was named Abbot. In the following year, 1765, by an ukase of March 7, Sanaxar was officially classified as a monastery, not a hermitage."*

Due to the increase in the number of brethren, they had to think about the construction of a new, large stone church in place of the older and smaller wooden one. They began to seek the permission of Bishop Pachomius of Tambov in 1767. When the footings for the foundation had been dug, and a Moleben had been sung at the placing of the foundation, a swarm of bees flew nearby (it is not known from whence) and settled on that spot where the high place in the altar was to be. This clearly signified the increase of the brethren and abundance of grace for those living in the monastery. "Fr. Theodore commanded Fr. Herman** to brush them into the hive and from that time there have been bees in the monastery."***

At one time His Eminence Pachomius, Bishop of Tambov, summoned

---

* *Biography and Teachings of the Elder Hieromonk Theodore (Ushakov), Restorer and Abbot of Sanaxar Monastery* (Temnikov: Sanaxar Monastery, 1992), pp. 8-9.

** It is assumed that this Herman was the future Saint of Alaska.

*** From the "Stories of Fr. Theophan about His Own Life and the Ascetics of His Time," in N. Subbotin, *Archimandrite Theophan, Abbot of the St. Cyril of New Lake Monastery* (St. Petersburg: *Strannik,* 1862), p. 58. In another edition of these same notes, the identity of this brother is given as Fr. Gerasim. Elsewhere right after this account, in the same memoirs about Sarov and Sanaxar, he mentions, "Fr. Herman who is now in America." We know from St. Herman of Alaska's own words that he had dear friends from both Sarov and Sanaxar and therefore we can see in Elder Theodore one of the earliest instructors of St. Herman of Alaska. See his "Letter No. 2, To Abbot Nazarius," in *Little Russian Philokalia,* Volume III (Platina, California: St. Herman of Alaska Brotherhood, 1989), p. 159. This relationship was evidently not known to the editors of the history of the evangelization of Alaska, but, nonetheless, in the introduction to that volume credit is given chiefly to Elder Theodore of Sanaxar for the spiritual revival that preceded the American Mission in the 18th century. See *An Historical Outline of the American Orthodox Spiritual Mission (Kadiak Mission 1794-1837)* (St. Petersburg: Valaam Monastery, 1894).

the Elder and said, "Fr. Theodore, as you have plenty of monks, while I have a lack of them, give me as many as will be needed."*

Fr. Theodore answered, "Your Eminence, my monks have entrusted their souls to me, and hence such a separation will be sorrowful and harmful for them. Wouldn't Your Eminence be just as pleased to take monks from a monastery where they have incomparably more than we do?"

To this the Bishop said, "I hesitated to conscript anyone from Sarov Monastery, for there the brethren are tonsured through the efforts of His Eminence Demetrius Sechenov."

Fr. Theodore enjoined, "With us, Your Eminence, the monks are tonsured by Imperial decree."

Although the Bishop was angered by such an answer, he decided not to take anyone.

7. MONASTIC LIFE IN SANAXAR

Two brothers, who had not long before entered the monastery and were not steadfast in the faith, once came to Fr. Theodore concerning their thoughts. One of them said, "Permit me, holy Father, during the present long winter nights to have a fire in my cell because of my despondency, for illumination and the reading of books." The Elder said to him, "In place of the material light which you demand, learn to seek the light of heaven, the noetic light. In my monastery, outside of the refectory, beginners are not allowed to have books in their cells, because they will appropriate from them not so much that which is useful for the soul but, on the contrary, will accustom themselves to giving commentaries to the spoiling of their soul's salvation, thinking that not they, but others do not live in such a way."

The other brother said, "A thought inclines me to the secluded life of the desert, to abandon the common life of obedience." The Elder replied to

---

*Bishops would regularly request the assistance of monks from nearby monasteries in managing and serving in the Archbishop's residence, administering diocesan affairs and serving in vacant parishes. Bishops would often view monks as expendable. Elder Theodore, on the contrary, saw monasticism as renunciation of the world to achieve union with God and association with bishops as a temptation to the love of authority and ambition and the conscription of monks by bishops as foreign to the aim of the monastic life.

him, "Remember how much the fathers of ancient times, living in seclusion, suffered from self-opinion, while others even fell into heresy and many of them remained forever incorrigible and perished. Beware, lest the Scripture be fulfilled in you that *Those who have no guidance fall like leaves* (Prov. 11:14) and, again, *Woe to him that is alone when he falleth* into despondency (Eccl. 4:10) for who shall raise him up? The Holy Fathers judged that a person who has entered the monastic life be under fatherly obedience without fail, which is called a life of suffering. In time he will receive great mercy from the Lord God and will be crowned with wreaths of glory equal with the martyrs and confessors of Christ."

After this he added, "Whoever wishes to live in seclusion with my blessing must endure a three-year trial with me in the coenobium. Every annoyance and humiliation that happens to you from others must be borne with love. Your food must be bread and cabbage soup, and that but once a day. You must take part in every obedience and appear before everyone else. If you bear such a three-year trial without murmuring, then I will bless you to live in seclusion. A brother desiring the desert life, who accepts whatever rule is given to him from his father, but cannot endure it, must therefore remain in the common life in obedience, repenting for his former self-rule." In such a manner, the Elder corrected both brothers.

Archimandrite Theophan (Sokolov) of New Lake, once a novice under Elder Theodore, wrote, "I entered the monastic life at eighteen years of age. Earlier I had thought of leaving the world, but I had to set aside my plans. Then, as the plague began (in 1771), I made ready quickly. I will tell you how we made our beginning (that is, our first attempts in the monastic life). We sought to learn where to find the strictest life. We chose to go to the monastery where the service was longest—Sarov Monastery. But no, there it was still lax! We went to Fr. Theodore in Sanaxar. The monastery was without a wall, encircled by a fence. The church was small with little sash widows, the walls inside were not finished, and there was little light. We read in church with splinters.*

"The clothing we wore! White smocks! There was a plain gray cassock

---

* They were too poor to afford candles so they burned splinters in order to read the service books. These splinters would smoke terribly and cause their eyes to water and the smoke would irritate their lungs.

for one person, for whomever was sent to town to buy supplies. In the beginning we suffered deprivations, and it was difficult! We walked around in bast shoes*—some were woven [tightly] from small pieces and others [loosely] from large pieces. We slept similarly—one hut was smaller, another was larger. Our legs were wrapped with leggings of the coarsest woven flax, but we did not walk barefoot. A brother—who himself had the key—came to Fr. Theodore and said, 'Bless me to pick out some bast shoes.' He told the brother to pick them out himself. Having picked the ones made with small strips of bark (ie., the better ones), Fr. Theodore called out to him, 'Come here,' and he took them away from him. This happened to Fr. Ignatius. The Elder took away the closely woven shoes and scolded him for being tempted by shoes. And Ignatius was from the palace nobility! The brothers began to say: 'You endure and endure, yet you receive no consolation here, not even in bast shoes!' Fr. Theodore heard this and called out: 'What's going on there?' 'Well, Elder, look what trouble there is, and you don't even allow any consolation in this.' He began to present the matter to them: 'What sense does this make? Why do you want to lose your salvation over such a small trifle?'

"I shared a cell with Macarius. He experienced more trials than anyone from Fr. Theodore. Fr. Theodore deliberately tested the brethren and therefore he would give poorly sewn smocks, with long backs or with lots of patches, to whomever loved to pick out their own clothing. He gave one such smock to Fr. Macarius. The latter came to Fr. Theodore upset and showed how the robe did not fit him—how the back did not fit. Fr. Theodore began to exhort him, 'Why did you come to the monastery? Did you do so consciously? What do you spend your time doing? You're depriving yourself of God's mercy! What are you concerned about? Rags! It would be better if you were busy cleansing your soul so that you would not be passionate about something temporal!' Afterwards, they would grow used to them.

"In order that no one might have anything of his own, there wasn't anything! No one ever had a fire in his cell. I performed such obediences as washing the floors, collecting kindling, washing the spoons and cooking the food.

---

*Shoes made from woven strips of birch bark which were worn by the common people.

We would stand guard at night, walk around, make several prostrations to the ground and pray.

"Twice during the time that I was there, Fr. Ignatius fled to the bishop. After he had been ordained a hierodeacon, Fr. Ignatius would dampen his hair in the evening, braid it, and afterwards comb it out. He would put on an ironed sticharion, but wear bast shoes! While standing on the ambon, Fr. Theodore beckoned to him. 'You, are a peacock,' he said. 'You have spread your tail feathers, but look at your legs. Go, take off that sticharion!' The latter was hurt and fled during the night to Bishop Jerome to complain that he had been embarrassed and put to shame. But the bishop sent him back to Fr. Theodore to be assigned a penance of prostrations.

"Fr. Theodore didn't keep any of the brethren in the monastery by force, and would say, 'The gates are open for anyone who chooses to leave.' He could not tolerate the words, 'I don't want to,' and couldn't listen to them."*

8. HOLY DISCERNMENT

One time Fr. Theodore, seated with the brethren in the refectory on the Feast of the Annunciation of the Most Holy Theotokos, was conversing with landowners who had come to this feast. He said, "Listen, my friends, what the Holy Church declares in the hymns of the present feast—*Let every mortal born on earth, carrying his torch, in spirit leap for joy* (Irmos, ode nine, Feast of the Annunciation), and cry out with one another, for the fount of God's greatest mercy is poured out on us in the Incarnation of His Only-begotten Son, the Savior of the world. It says, *Announce, O earth, tidings of great joy.* One must understand here that under the name 'earth,' not the earth but the people living on it are charged to proclaim this joy. May the earth be filled with this proclamation, and pious Christian souls with spiritual joy. But tell me, can a soul occupied with the merriments of this age

---

*From the "Stories of Fr. Theophan about His Own Life and the Ascetics of His Time," in N. Subbotin, *Archimandrite Theophan, Abbot of the St. Cyril of New Lake Monastery* (St. Petersburg: *Strannik,* 1862), pp. 57-58.

feel this joy? It seems to me that since man cannot serve both God and mammon, so, too, it is impossible for one occupied with temporal delights to feel spiritual joy in God."

When the Elder went to his cell after the meal in the refectory, one of his guests asked his permission to come to him for his spiritual needs. Fr. Theodore invited him. There, among other things, the nobleman asked him, "If a man living in the world is not to take pleasure in the good things of this age, then why has God produced so many beautiful things on earth? I cannot understand how God, being One, has given us two commandments so totally at variance. According to one commandment everything on the earth is beautiful. Everything that He created good He gives for food and our use, and to that end everything was created exceedingly good. But, according to the other commandment, He requires of man fasting and continence. I ask you, Your Reverence, explain this to me and resolve my perplexity."

Fr. Theodore replied to this, "Why speak and interpret these mysteries hidden from us? God cannot be unjust, and whatever He says in His Omniscience, He says truly. Our task is to obey the truth without contradiction. These two commandments were given even in Paradise—*And God commanded Adam saying, Of every tree in paradise thou mayest eat; but of the tree of the knowledge of good and evil, thou shalt not eat of it: for in the day that thou eatest thereof, thou shalt die the death* (Gen 2:16-17). It is apparent that fasting is akin to man's nature. But, if—out of need of fasting—God did not will to create in such abundance all of the goods of the earth, then fasting would be involuntary for everyone. Thus one should think that the abundance of the good things of the earth is not for delight but for the perfection of fasting. God did not will an involuntary fast, but wished that we—in the midst of this abundance—not only remain continent but also fast according to our own will out of love for Him, as handed down by the Holy Church. For obedience to this law He has promised us in reward—health of body and salvation of soul; and, for disobedience—death. If, at the same time, abundance were not given to the earth, then what kind of consolation could there be for the weak, those sick in body, the aged, and infants? For their sake, God has not confined us all to want, but has been pleased that our abundance can fulfill the requirement of each." Hearing this, the guest was at peace and went on his way, thanking Fr. Theodore for his profitable conversation and for solving his uncertainties.

A certain brother informed the Abbot that people working under contract on the building of the church and other projects had been acquiring surplus money, and expressed the fear that after the completion of the work it would not be possible to take it from them. To this, Fr. Theodore said: "They are poor people, my friend. Let this surplus take the place of alms for them."

Once, not far from the monastery, the monastery mill caught fire and everything burned. The loss of everything, including the structure, was valued at 500 roubles. The brother responsible for the fire, not knowing how to answer for this due to his unexpected sorrow, dared not to appear before Fr. Theodore. When several brothers conducted him to the Abbot, then the Elder, with his usual love of man, didn't punish him even in word but only exclaimed like Job: *The Lord hath given and the Lord hath taken away, as the Lord hath willed, so let it be* (Job 1:21).

This mill had been built to grind wheat and for crushing tree bark to sell. The Elder taught that one must obtain one's own bread by means of one's labor, for which reason, among other tasks, certain brothers sewed mittens and sold them in the city.

9. THE ARZAMAS SISTERS

Whenever it happened that fish were caught in the fishing holes belonging to the monastery, the Elder would always set aside nearly half of what was caught, saying, "This is for my poor unfortunate ones." These [unfortunate ones] should be understood as the sisters under his direction in the abolished Arzamas Alexeyevsky Convent, the lay workers—both widows and virgins—and the community of those who entrusted their souls to him. Fr. Theodore took vigilant care for their salvation and welfare. The diocesan bishop gave him a blessing to visit this convent. For this reason, he left Sanaxar Monastery for the city of Arzamas two—and sometimes three—times a year.

Travelling to Arzamas, he usually stopped at the *metochion** of the

---

* A branch or outpost of a monastery situated in a city, town or countryside where monks would reside while conducting necessary business or performing tasks for the monastery.

Sanaxar Monastery. From there, he usually went to the Alexeyevsky Convent at an appropriate time during the day. At every arrival, he was met by the sisters as by his own children, with faces filled with spiritual joy. He would then usually enter their large common cell and, after partaking with them of material food, would pour forth to them a spring of spiritual discourse on the Lord. He would freely give to each a reassuring solution to all of the spiritual needs which she expressed, conversing at times even until Vespers. After this, he would travel back to spend the night at the metochion. During long talks he would sometimes get a cough resulting from an internal illness which had once befallen him due to his excessive fasting and continence in the wilds. As a result, he could barely eat at night. The Elder would spend a week or two in Arzamas for these soul-saving activities and then return again to his monastery.

The following rule had been appointed to be observed in the convent by Fr. Theodore. Everything was to be held in common. All were in obedience to the Mother Superior and were to have a pure conscience and always reveal to her what troubled them. The Mother Superior, as their true mother, was to maintain motherly care for all, not loving one more than another, but showing equal love and regard to everyone. Whatever defective moral characteristics appeared, she was to correct with long-suffering and meekness. Uncertainties which she could not resolve were to be referred to the Elder's discretion. Every sister would be given an obedience and task suited to her character, from which she could acquire her daily bread. Their handicrafts were diverse—some sewed clothes brought by civilians, others spun yarn, embroidered with gold thread, threaded pearls, wove cloth, and knitted stockings. They usually labored all day. Sometimes they would sit at their tasks until quite late in the evening, while one sister would read a book aloud to them. In the evening, at the ringing of a bell, they would gather for the meal in the large common refectory.

After fortifying themselves bodily with whatever food they had obtained from their labor, they would gather in that same room to read Vespers, Compline, and the three canons (to Sweetest Jesus, to the Most Holy Theotokos and to the Guardian Angel), and all together would say the Jesus Prayer 100 times with 50 prostrations, the prayers of commemoration (benefactors both living and dead), and the evening prayers. These prayers, as well as the reading during the meals and other reading, were read in turn by those sisters who were literate. Being attentive to the reader, the rest would pray. After the rule and having asked forgiveness, they would then disperse with prayer to their cells. In the middle of the night, after not more than five hours of rest, all the sisters would gather together again in the common cell to conduct the morning prayer services. They would read the morning prayers, the prayers of commemoration and a kathisma. Afterwards, each went to do her handiwork which she continued until the midday meal. On ordinary days, they would take turns going to the church along with those who were dispensable from their obediences and with the elderly. On feast days, they would all walk together and stand in a special place behind a partition erected in accordance with Fr. Theodore's wise fatherly discretion, hidden from the sight of laymen.

Since they lived together by tens due to the great number of sisters, they were given a commandment from their Elder that, except for a rare necessary word, one was not to speak to another—one was to say nothing personally and, even more so, to say nothing in annoyance, nor give an opportunity to express an opinion, either by a glance or by a gesture. Everything among them would be done, according to the apostolic teaching, out of love, since our salvation comes from our neighbor. Except for ten elderly sisters appointed to make the necessary purchases, no one was to go out of the monastery. Others, who had been living in the monastery for twenty years, deprived themselves of every worldly consolation and continued in patience, hoping for recompense in the future life which God has prepared for those who love Him.

10. THE ELDRESS OF KIEV, ST. DOSITHEA

In Sanaxar it happened that two brother laborers who had come to live in the monastery not long before, were scandalized that one Father would maintain two monasteries—one for men, the other for women—supposing in their thoughts that two monasteries could not have a sole shepherd. They revealed this to the Elder. He tried to help them understand by means of

Eldress Dosithea of the Kiev Caves Lavra.

many explanations but they clung to their opinions and asked Fr. Theodore to let them go for an answer to the Schema-monk Dositheus,* renowned at that time for living a virtuous life in the Kiev Caves Lavra. The Elder willingly blessed them to go. Having come to Fr. Dositheus in Kiev, they revealed their doubts. They said that Fr. Theodore had two monasteries, a men's and a women's, under his governance.

"Did you notice any weaknesses in him?" the recluse asked.

"No, he lives a strict life."

"What shortcomings exist there?"

"There aren't any."

"What do you take him to be?"

"A saint."

"Is he literate?"

"He's well educated."

"Why do you have doubts? Have none. A smart head can shepherd not only two flocks, but even ten!"

Thus were they set at ease.**

Having told them much else to their benefit, he ordered them to return to Fr. Theodore. In such a way, having resolved their doubts, they came back to the Elder.

11. THE TEACHER OF THE MONASTIC LIFE

Once, Fr. Theodore happened to be in the capital city of Moscow, where he spent about two months in order to straighten out certain monastery needs. During this time people of every background came to him out of their fervor and for profit to their soul. Noblemen invited him to dine almost everyday, dispatching horses to bring him. At one noblemen's residence he

---

*The Schema-monk Dositheus here mentioned was in actuality a woman. Schema-nun Dosithea was canonized as a Saint by the Orthodox Church in 1993 together with a group of other ascetics from the Kiev region. St. Paisius Velichkovsky also sent some of his disciples to this great woman ascetic. It was she who sent St. Seraphim to live the ascetic life in Sarov.

** From the "Stories of Fr. Theophan about His Own Life and the Ascetics of His Time," in N. Subbotin, *Archimandrite Theophan, Abbot of the St. Cyril of New Lake Monastery* (St. Petersburg: *Strannik*, 1862), pp. 58-59.

happened to dine in this way with certain spiritual leaders and abbots of Moscow. There was a conversation among them concerning monastic dress. The Moscow fathers said that in the reigning city they were forbidden to wear clothing made of simple and cheap material and asked Fr. Theodore what he thought about this. Fr. Theodore told them, "You could have a blessed justification for yourselves, holy fathers, if during the tonsure before the Gospel you had given your vows concerning the enduring of poverty according to some other rules. But, since the rite of tonsure is one and the vows are the same, not much commentary is needed. To interpret and relax this in accordance with the passions, will—in its own time—be unto one's judgment. It is not fitting for spiritual people to have luxurious clothing, private servants, worldly hairstyles or fancy carriages which display ostentation. A monk is not a worldly lord, but a person who has died to the world, even though he be a Superior."

They were not able to raise objections against this.

At one time, while Fr. Theodore was in Moscow, one of his disciples was sent on an obedience to conduct monastery business on Dmitrovskaya Street. He went to the St. George Convent to church for the Liturgy. After the Liturgy, the Abbess of this monastery invited him to have a cup of tea with her. But this disciple replied, "Since my Elder is here in Moscow, I may not come to your cell without his blessing." Then the Abbess in amazement could not refrain from saying aloud to all her sisters in church, "Listen, sisters, to what this novice said—'I cannot go to your cell without my Elder's blessing.'" And later, still repeating these words, she added, "That is how real monks live." Having received such edification from that novice's obedience, the Abbess and sisters dispersed to their cells.

When Fr. Theodore returned to Sanaxar Monastery, two disciples came to him—one of them had grown weak from a longing for his parents and relatives induced on him by the demons, while the other was disturbed by the horrors and fears inflicted on him at night by the demons and, sorrowing over this, had disclosed it to the Elder. He said to the first of them, "Friend, endure your sorrow for your parents and your patience will be rewarded from the Lord God in His time. Likewise, if your parents and relatives, who are grieving over you, bear this good-heartedly, they will be recompensed in the future life." To the one disturbed by fear he said, "You must go, my friend, to the place where the fear occurs, making the sign of the Cross and praying. Whoever does this cannot be harmed in the least by the demons."

Two other brothers came as well to the Elder in his cell and the first said, "Because of despondency, holy Father, I have the desire to learn the Psalms of David by heart. I have already learned several of them by heart without your blessing, for which I ask forgiveness." And the other said, "Because of my weakness, life in this monastery is unbearable for me, holy father. Thus, am I disposed in thought to go to another place." The Elder said to the first, who had memorized some of the Psalms, "I cannot forbid anyone to occupy themselves in this soul-profiting task, but on the contrary, I further support you according to the word of the Holy Apostle Paul: *Let the Word of Christ dwell in you richly in all wisdom, ... admonishing* you *in psalms and hymns and spiritual songs, singing with grace in your hearts to the Lord* (Col. 3:16). To the other one he said, "Do you wish to find God on the easy path? What further labors should you bear for God? Be ashamed of your faintheartedness, my friend! Do you see what torments the holy martyrs suffered? One could spend two hundred years in such a life like ours without suffering as the Holy Martyrs suffered for only a short time in their torments."

12. PREMATURE DESIRE FOR THE DESERT LIFE

One time, three novices of his ascetic flock came to Fr. Theodore's cell and began to ask him to allow them to go to the desert for the most perfect life [of seclusion]. He would not permit them to do so, and in every way possible tried to instruct them to abandon this undertaking, which was not to their profit. But he was not able to succeed with his profitable instructions. Knowing how dangerous it is to go into the wilderness if one has not learned humility, the Elder wanted to alarm them by means of fear. With this aim, after the refectory meal and having detained the brethren, he began to speak: "Whoever wants to go live in the wilderness stand on one side and whoever wants to live in obedience on the other," and no one was found desiring to go live in the woods except those three brothers. Approaching them he said, "When you go, know that you are going of your own will and without a blessing. I am not giving you a blessing, so that I will not be responsible for your perdition."

In spite of this, and being stubborn, they remained firm in their resolve and went into the wilderness. But such disobedience had miserable consequences. Not one of them remained in the desert. The enemy led one to the world and he married. Another he instructed to go to his father's house in order to lead a life like that of St. Alexis, the Man of God, and urged on by zeal for great fasting, he was led to feeblemindedness and was inclined by some Old-Ritualists into schism.* The third cut off his hand to further demonstrate the unheard-of example of fulfilling literally the words of Christ—*if thy hand offend thee, cut it off* (cf. Matt. 18:8). In the meantime, the Elder and the brothers did not cease praying for them. And the Lord did not deprive them in the end of His grace. Having become very poor in life, the first re-entered the spiritual life after his wife's death and died as a hieromonk in the Tikhvin Monastery. The second was corrected by a brother of the Sanaxar Monastery, who had come to him at the time of his death. He died in repentance and was buried as a monastery laborer in the city of Kineshma near a church. The third was taken to Valaam Monastery and ended his life as a monk.** In this way, the desert life—begun prematurely, out of self-will and without blessing—was not to the advantage of any of them.

13. SPIRITUAL DIRECTION OF LAYMEN

Once, several noblemen came to the monastery to receive the blessing of Fr. Theodore and his spiritual instructions. Amid the conversations they asked: "How should we treat our evil-mannered servants, holy father? We consider it a sin to punish them for, as the Scripture says, *Whoever wishes to be great among you, let him be the servant of all* (cf. Mark 10:43–44), and *He who humbles himself shall be exalted* (Luke 18:14). For this reason, one should

---

*Old-Ritualists (or Old-Believers) broke communion with the Orthodox Church in Russia over liturgical reforms hastily promulgated during the time of Patriarch Nikon in the seventeenth century. Despite governmental persecution they survived in some rural regions. They have historically set themselves apart by their tendency toward extremes and sectarian expression, although they have preserved well the Church's ancient traditions.

** See section 25 of this Life.

think that we landlords must behave toward our serfs like fathers and not beat them even if there be cause. The queen bee serves as an image of this, since she has no stinger."

The Elder answered them: "You have set for yourselves a good rule, to strive to seek instruction from others in spiritual matters. The Sacred Scripture has much literal, historical and allegorical wisdom, which it is not given to everyone to explain. Every recorded prophecy does not happen just as it is narrated, for in actual fact in the beginning it had not yet taken place. The Ethiopian Queen's eunuch, reading the book of the Prophet Isaiah, would not have understood what he had read if Philip, the Apostle of Christ, had not instructed him (Acts 8:26-35). Thus I tell you, my friends, it is good that you have asked how you should be disposed to your ill-mannered serfs.

"Listen to what the Holy Fathers teach concerning this. If one does not correct evil manners nor punish the incorrigible, it would be impossible for good people to live on the earth, as St. John Chrysostom reasons about this in his discourses. He says that if 'you were to deprive the city of its rulers and fear of magistrates be wholly taken away, then both houses and cities would be destroyed. People unhindered by fear of punishment would destroy one another, biting and devouring one another—the rich man the poorer, the stronger man the weaker.'* In the Book of Kings it is mentioned that the Old Testament priest Eli, although he reproached his own sons verbally for their licentious actions yet, because he did not punish them physically, he himself was severely punished by God (I Kings 2:12-4:11).

"With the coming of the grace-filled state, Christ the Savior Who is the model of life to everyone, though He did say, *For I am meek and lowly in heart* (Matt: 11:29) yet, in cases which demanded it, He required severity. Thus more than once did He take a whip and cast the disorderly money changers out of the temple. In conversations with His disciples, He would sometimes use gentle words, and other times harsh words. One time, for example, He praised Peter, *Blessed art thou, Simon Bar Jona* (Matt 16:17) and promised to found the Church on his confession. A little while after these words, He severely rebuked him saying, *Get thee behind me Satan, thou art an offence unto*

---

*"The Homilies on the Statutes to the People of Antioch," in *Nicene and Post-Nicene Fathers,* Volume IX (Grand Rapids: Eerdmans Publishing Co., 1983), Homily Six, p. 381.

me (Matt 16:23). At another time, He said to them all, *Are ye also yet without understanding?* (Matt. 15:16). Remember also the words of the holy Apostle Jude, *Of some, have compassion, making a difference: others save with fear* (Jude 1:22,23).

"St. John Chrysostom, in his homilies on the Epistle of the Apostle to the Galatians, in chapter one, says not only to worldly authorities, but also to spiritual shepherds, 'To always address one's disciples with mildness, even when they need severity, is not the part of a teacher but would be more the part of a corrupter and enemy.'* Thus, every bodily punishment should be carried out with moderation, not in order to satisfy one's revenge and evil passion, nor violating Christian humility.

"Remember what happened during the time of the Grand Prince Vladimir. When he began to show his people excessive favors after baptism and set his strictness aside, great confusion resulted from this among the people, and because they led evil lives they did not become good people. This compelled St. Vladimir to institute civil laws. When a surgeon amputates a person's decaying arm or leg, he is not destroying that person but bringing about his health. One should likewise evaluate the punishment of the guilty." After such a conversation the noblemen left his cell with their doubts resolved and their souls contented.

14. A SHEEP GOES ASTRAY

A certain Nilov [according to other documents, Neyelov], a Temnikov Voyevod,** wished to have Fr. Theodore as his confessor and asked him about this diligently. Fr. Theodore said that he would not agree to be his confessor except under the condition that he, in regard to everything for his soul's profit, would unfailingly follow his instruction, according to the word of the Holy Apostle Paul to the Holy Apostle Timothy, *Preach the word; be instant in season, out of season; reprove, rebuke, exhort with all longsuffering and doctrine* (II Tim. 4:2). The Voyevod was disposed to be obedient to

---

* "Commentary on the Epistle of St. Paul to the Galatians," in *Nicene and Post-Nicene Fathers,* Volume XIII (Grand Rapids: Eerdmans Publishing Co., 1983), Chapter One, p. 1.

** *Voyevod*: a military official.

him in everything, as a son to his father, and continued to carry this out for three years without any opposition. In the end, he became disobedient. He began to disregard the fasts and the fast days. In the city during the summer, he sealed the stoves of the citizens. If someone wished a stove to be unsealed he would have to pay a rouble per stove. Affairs began to be resolved unfairly for bribes. The innocent were blamed, while the guilty were acquitted. Hearing many complaints, and zealous to exhort him, Fr. Theodore severely reproached the Voyevod. But he considered these reproaches of Fr. Theodore to be nothing. Finally, he compelled the peasants to build his country house during the harvest season. The peasants begged Fr. Theodore to come and personally persuade the Voyevod to give them time to gather the grain.

"Seeing such oppression, Fr. Theodore travelled to the city of Temnikov which was two miles from the monastery, and came to the Voyevod's residence. Hearing of this, the Voyevod went to his office, sat behind his legal desk and summoned Fr. Theodore. When he entered, the Voyevod authoritatively asked what need he had of him. Fr. Theodore recapped all of the Voyevod's deeds and urged him to stop his looting and oppression of the poor. The Voyevod ordered his secretary to record word for word that the Superior of the Sanaxar Monastery had, on official record, declared him to be a robber. He afterwards presented this to the Governor of Voronezh. The Governor, in turn, reported this to Empress Catherine II and she sent the Synod an order to investigate this affair. For this reason the governor was ordered to summon Fr. Theodore [to Voronezh] and take down his reply. Fr. Theodore then took me (Fr. Theophan) along with him to write a reply."*

At a certain point on the road to Voronezh, in the village of Bolshie Talinka, not eighteen miles from Tambov, there lived a certain Deacon Michael Nikiforov, a spiritual son of Fr. Theodore, who strictly fulfilled all his father's instructions. On both legs of Fr. Theodore's journey, there and back, the deacon met his instructor with great reverence. At the same time, he introduced him to a great number of parishioners of both sexes—the old and

---

*Postscript to *The Life of Fr. Theodore, former Abbot of the Sanaxar Monastery* (Moscow, 1847).

the young, wives and virgins—whom he had won over to the spiritual life at the Elder's instruction. They wept when he addressed his teachings to them. Likewise, when Fr. Theodore was preparing to leave, they saw him off with tears and, out of their regard for him, brought him everything they could and placed it at his feet.

These villagers, who had undertaken the spiritual life, lived lovingly with one another, more closely than relatives. They helped those who had nothing, providing them everything needful, and because of this they had sufficiency among themselves in every household item. Drunkenness and disorderly behavior had been totally uprooted in their village; neither were there unseemly songs or games, or grief, or carousing. God's church was always full of people, and incessant prayer from pure hearts was offered to the Lord God.

Complaints were made against this deacon by his enviers to the Governor-General Vorontsov, saying that he was propagating an unmarried way of life and was introducing what would become a sect and some sort of new doctrine. The Governor-General, bringing this to the attention of His Eminence Theodosius, Bishop of Tambov, asked him to investigate this affair. For this reason an investigative team was sent to the village, the deacon's books were confiscated and he was taken to the bishop. The bishop, examining the books, tested what the deacon taught, and after examining him said, "If all the clergy in my diocese were like that, then I would be saved by their prayers." After this, the deacon was released with gratitude by His Eminence and sent home.

15. ST. TIKHON OF ZADONSK

Having given his reply to the Governor-General, Fr. Theodore went from Voronezh to the Zadonsk Monastery where St. Tikhon,* the former bishop of Voronezh, was living in retirement. St. Tikhon had served as bishop of Voronezh for six years. The impact made upon him by the unjust defrocking of Metropolitan Arsenius (Matsievich) of Rostov led to his early retirement to Zadonsk Monastery, where he spent the last fourteen years of

---

*St. Tikhon of Zadonsk (1724–1783).

Metropolitan Arsenius (Matsievich) of Rostov in prison after his unjust
defrocking, dressed as a layman. On the wall beside him is a portrait
of him in his episcopal vestments.

his life writing Christian moral instructions for laymen and hundreds of letters of spiritual direction. He lived in a small house next to the bell tower. As Fr. Theodore entered the hierarch's cell he was struck by his simplicity which can be seen in the following description recorded by the bishop's cell attendant Basil.

"He had no bed, but only a small carpet and two pillows. He had no blankets, but used his coat of lambskin to keep himself warm at night. He had but one cassock, and it was made of coarse wool. There were no decorations in his cell, but only a few holy images representing our Savior's Passion and other Gospel scenes. Everything was in accordance with his humility of wisdom and his voluntary poverty."*

In describing his daily way of life, Basil adds, "At dinner it was his custom to listen to the Holy Scriptures of the Old Testament, which I would read aloud to him. But what was remarkable in him was his great and ardent love of God. He rarely sat at table without tears of contrition, especially when he was listening to the reading of the book of the Prophet Isaiah. Sometimes he would say, 'Read that chapter again,' and putting down his spoon, he would begin to weep."**

We do not know how well they had known one another beforehand, but St. Tikhon had been in continual contact with Abbot Ephraim of Sarov Monastery since shortly after the time of Fr. Theodore's arrival there in 1757. During his stay at Zadonsk Monastery, Elder Theodore enjoyed the most intimate fellowship with the holy hierarch. The latter received Fr. Theodore with great love. St. Tikhon knew well what lay ahead for the zealous ascetic for he, too, in retirement in the monastery, had suffered many offenses from the superiors, from worldly monks, and sometimes even from the lay workers who would laugh at him as he passed by. It was not only by outward gestures of asking forgiveness that he overcame evil by good, but above all in prayer to God, to the extent that he was able to consider such men as his benefactors. His cell-attendant describes his life of prayer as follows: "He was wont to

---

*Chebotarev, Basil Ivanov, "Memoirs by Chebotarev of the Life of St. Tychon of Zadonsk," *A Treasury of Russian Spirituality,* edited by G. P. Fedotov (London: Sheed and Ward, 1950), pp. 195-196.

**Ibid., p. 191.

City of Voronezh in the eighteenth century.

spend the night without sleep and lie down to rest at dawn. At night he exerted himself in prayer with prostrations. These prayers were not cold, but were filled with the greatest fervor, proceeding from a contrite heart, so that sometimes he would cry aloud, 'Lord, have mercy! Lord spare me!...' and he would beat his head on the ground. All this was wrought in him by the fiery love of God within him. As the hour of midnight struck, he would go into the anteroom of his cell, chanting the holy psalms in a gentle and contrite voice."*

A benefactor of widows, a father and protector of orphans, he was a consoler to all in distress and misfortunes. He considered as lost any day that passed in which he was not able to give alms. It was his custom to frequently travel to the nearby city of Elets under the pretext of visiting friends, but

---

*Ibid., p. 192.

51

would leave his carriage across the river and walk to the prison on foot. "Entering, he would greet everyone as if they were his own children, would sit with them, inquiring of each about the cause of his imprisonment. Trying their conscience, he would first console, then exhort them to an awareness of their crime, to repentance, to nobly bearing their fetters. Departing, he would offer them alms, and to those held because of debts, he would give money for bail...."*

On the first day of Pascha he could be found in prison greeting the inmates with the Resurrection of Christ, unfailingly greeting each prisoner with the Paschal kiss and saying, "Christ is Risen!"

The days spent with St. Tikhon were arranged by God's Providence to give encouragement to Elder Theodore and he could not have found another man who at that moment could have given him the proper counsel for the trials that loomed ahead. These words written by St. Tikhon would certainly have fallen on good soil in the heart of the Elder who, for righteousness' sake, had fallen from favor.

"If you are exiled, think of the convicts, who in rags and half-naked are estranged from their native places, who are beaten daily, whose days are spent in forced labor, whose nights are passed in dark, filthy and stinking dungeons, who remain without any comfort and who yet endure."**

"If there is any rest in this world, then it consists only in purity of the conscience and patience. This is a harbor for us who sail upon the sea of life.... But true, eternal and undisturbed rest is stored up for us in eternal life, for which reason it is called *rest* in the Scriptures(cf. Heb. 4:11), which I desire for both you and myself—the restless Tikhon."***

St. Tikhon's disciples said that he had never been so happy with another guest as with this guest—Fr. Theodore. The spiritual exchange

---

* *Life of Our Father among the Saints Tikhon, Bishop of Voronezh, Wonderworker of All Russia,* 2nd ed. (St. Petersburg, 1862).

** Gorodetzky, Nadejda, *St. Tikhon Zadonsky, Inspirer of Dostoevsky* (London: SPCK, 1950), p. 109.

*** Letter 32, Tikhon Zadonskii, St., *Works of Our Father among the Saints Tikhon of Zadonsk* (Gregg International Pub., 1970); cited in *Life of Our Father among the Saints Tikhon, Bishop of Voronezh, Wonderworker of All Russia,* 2nd ed. (St. Petersburg, 1862), p. 77.

St. Tikhon of Zadonsk visiting prisoners on Pascha.
Illustration from *The Russian Pilgrim,* 1903.

between them went on for three days. Then, upon his departure, His Eminence deigned to conduct Fr. Theodore on his way through the entire monastery, even as far as the holy gates, and upon parting bowed extremely low to him.

16. BANISHMENT TO SOLOVKI

This famous, northernmost Lavra of Holy Russia was a fifteenth-century monastic citadel where great ascetics worked out their salvation. In the seventeenth century, the monastics were held captive by militant ultra-conservative forces during a fierce Old-Believer's uprising, which was eventually brought under control by Peter I. Orders were to keep the monastery as a fort against foreign invaders and Old-Believer schismatics. Thus, it also served as a prison for such great men as St. Joshua, the founder of Golgotha Skete.

Soon after Fr. Theodore's arrival at the Sanaxar Monastery a royal edict was sent by courier. It was ordered that Fr. Theodore be sent as an incorrigible troublemaker to the Solovki Monastery prison and all his belongings be sent with him in trunks once they had been registered.* This happened in 1774, although years earlier Elder Theodore had earned the respect and favor of the Empress, Abbot Ioasaph of the Arzamas Monastery of the Savior arrived to officially catalog his belongings. "Fr. Theodore showed them his belongings: a mat of cattle hair—woven like thick sackcloth, a small pillow stuffed with the same hair, a sheepskin hat, a mantle and riassa, and said, 'Register it all!' Those who had come from the city, having noted this all down in brief words, submitted the list where it was required."** Fr. Theodore set out for the Solovki Monastery prison, taking with him a felt mat and pillow. At his departure, his disciples from Sanaxar and his female disciples from Arzamas escorted him with great grief.

---

* "This Theodore, deprived of both the rank of Abbot and Hieromonk, is to be exiled as a simple monk, for being a troublesome person, to the Solovetsky Monastery. The Superior of that monastery is entrusted with diligent supervision over him." *Life of our Holy Father St. Theodore of Sanaxar* (Sanaxar Monastery, 1999), p. 43.

** Postscript to *The Life of Fr. Theodore, former Abbot of the Sanaxar Monastery* (Moscow, 1847), p.63.

View of Solovki Monastery, mid-1990s.

17. PUGACHEV'S UPRISING

A week after his departure, Pugachev's* band came to the city of Temnikov and looted the city. Archimandrite Theophan (Sokolov) adds to the Life of Elder Theodore the following account.

"I was also a witness of the fate that eventually befell the Voyevod Nilov. After the passage of only a week following the banishment of Fr. Theodore to Solovki Monastery, Pugachev's band came to the city. The Voyevod left town with great haste, taking all his money with him. However, travelling by Sanaxar Monastery, he repented that he had

---

*Emilian Pugachev, a Cossack who led a revolt during the reign of Catherine II. He was eventually captured near Astrakhan. Pushkin describes him in the novel *The Captain's Daughter*.

Emilian Pugachev, leader of a rebellion
in 1773.

sinned before Fr. Theodore, and travelled in haste to the Shatsk area with
his retinue.

"But inasmuch as Nilov came to Shatsk without informing anyone
who he was, he caused a great commotion in the town, for they thought
that Pugachev's band had come. He was fined because of this and also because he had left his city undefended. In a short while, he died there in
Shatsk, having publicly repented of the evil he had committed against the
Elder. Pugachev's band destroyed and plundered his city, but they sent
word to Sanaxar not to be afraid. At that time, I (Fr. Theophan) had not
left the monastery, although others—in no small numbers—had fled into
the forest. But they returned upon hearing that Pugachev's band would not
come to the monastery."*

---

* *The Life of Fr. Theodore, Former Abbot of the Sanaxar Monastery* (Moscow, 1847), pp.
63-64.

18. ST. PAISIUS VELICHKOVSKY

After Elder Theodore was banished, many of his disciples left. The majority of them went first to the Ostrovsky Hermitage of the Entrance of the Theotokos, to the renowned Elder Cleopas, who had previously lived on Mount Athos and with St. Paisius Velichkovsky. Then, many of these fathers continued on to Moldavia–Wallachia to the great Elder Paisius, Abbot of the Secu and Neamts Monasteries*.

We do not know how well St. Paisius was known in the neighboring Sarov and Sanaxar Monasteries. But in 1774, upon Elder Theodore's banishment to Solovki, and again in 1791 after his death, his spiritual children turned to St. Paisius, whom they knew to be a great monastic guide of the same caliber as their own Elder. St. Paisius, as well as his successors in Neamts, expressed the highest regard for Elder Theodore. Judging from his correspondence, it seems that he had detailed, firsthand knowledge of Elder Theodore, and that the men knew each other well. St. Paisius and Elder Theodore had both experienced the hardships of the monastic life and had been nurtured in the major monastic centers of their time. They knew from their own experience, not merely from the outward learning of books, the essence of the monastic tradition which they so effectively handed down to their disciples. The abbots and spiritual guides of the monastic centers in succeeding generations were primarily the offspring of these two fathers. In contrast to the dozens of pages left behind by Elder Theodore, Elder Paisius bequeathed to successive generations nearly an entire library, from his translations of ascetical and mystical literature to his own compositions on the question of the Baptism of Converts to the Orthodox Faith. Hence, it is only natural that the scattered flock and orphans of Elder Theodore would have recourse to St. Paisius—the great shepherd of Orthodox monasticism—for more of the rich food with which they had been nurtured.

---

* See section 24 of this Life.

Romanian icon of St. Paisius Velichkovsky.

19. LIFE AT SOLOVKI MONASTERY

During the entire nine years that Fr. Theodore lived in exile in the So-lovki Monastery, two monks from Sanaxar were sent to stay with him. Like-wise, sisters from Arzamas would travel carrying letters and requests for instructions, to which he, out of his fatherly love for them, always replied in order to instruct them, to assuage their sorrow of soul, and to spur them on to endurance of all the soul's afflictions which usually befall those journeying on the path to salvation. Similarly, he would reply separately to his disciples when one of them needed to resolve issues of conscience. Thus, one brother required the Elder's decision, since the Abbot was forcing him to accept the priestly rank of which he considered himself unworthy. Fr. Theodore ordered him not to resist but to obey and brought forward the example of many saints who, though once sinners and having afterwards become chaste, received the priesthood.

20. RETURN FROM BANISHMENT

In the end, after Fr. Theodore had lived as a prisoner on Solovki for nine years [1774-1783], God desired to return him again to his own monastery, to his disciples, where he had expended his labors. It came to pass in this way. One of his disciples*, after his Elder's banishment to Solovki, by God's unfathomable judgements, was conscripted as a cell-attendant for His Eminence Gabriel, Metropolitan of St. Petersburg. Compelled by his conscience to facilitate his Elder's return, and having this opportunity, he therefore informed His Eminence that Fr. Theodore was suffering unjustly, and asked him to do the favor of returning him from Solovki back to Sanaxar. His Eminence asked for a memorandum explaining what the whole affair was about. Insomuch as this cell-attendant had travelled together with Fr. Theodore to Voronezh for the documentation of the case, he knew the matter well, and without any difficulty he formulated a detailed brief.

On the basis of this memorandum His Eminence, being at the Palace for the Service of the Washing of the Feet on Great Thursday in 1783, explained the affair to the Sovereign Empress Catherine Alexeyevna [II] and assured her that Fr. Theodore was suffering unjustly, for his action had been totally misinterpreted in a way absolutely contrary to his intention. In the

---

*Archimandrite Theophan (Sokolov), Abbot of the St. Cyril of New Lake Monastery. A novice together with St. Herman of Alaska in the Sanaxar Monastery, he was later responsible for the appointment of Abbot Nazarius to Valaam Monastery and of many other spiritual men as heads of various monasteries in Russia. In a letter, St. Herman of Alaska asks that he be nominated Bishop of Alaska.

meantime Fr. Theodore, who had already been in Solovki for nine years, had suffered much from the cold air there and had fallen into great feebleness.

The Empress asked, "How old is he?"

The Metropolitan replied, "Some seventy years."

The Empress objected, "He couldn't be that old—I know him."

The next day, April 18, 1783, an Imperial edict was sent to His Eminence concerning the return of Fr. Theodore to whatever monastery he wished. The Metropolitan took this decree to the Holy Synod.

Consequently, it was decreed to return him to the Sanaxar Monastery. His Eminence informed Fr. Theodore in writing to come to Petersburg from Solovki to meet him. But Fr. Theodore could not travel to Petersburg since—due to his nine years of suffering on the Solovki Islands from the exceedingly cold air and from the heavy fumes in the cells [caused by smoke from the leaky stoves]—he felt great weakness. The cells were heated once or twice a week and the stoves were damped down too soon. From this, Fr. Theodore would become asphyxiated to such an extent that sometimes he would be taken out of the cell as one dead and they would revive him with snow. One of his disciples would be at hand at any given time, but as they were quartered in a distant cell, Fr. Theodore was subjected to such dangerous conditions.

So the Elder travelled directly from Solovki through Vologda, Yaroslavl, and Vladimir to Arzamas. When he arrived in Arzamas, he was met by two hieromonks of Sanaxar Monastery who awaited him there and by his disciples, the sisters of the Arzamas community. This was during the morning hymnody on October 9, 1783, and they received him with great joy. He gave his blessing to everyone and rejoiced with those rejoicing. Likewise, superiors from other monasteries came there to meet him, as well as respected lords and merchants, both men and women. Many of them invited him to visit their homes and offer spiritual instruction. For this reason he stayed a while in Arzamas, fulfilling their desires and requests. As a true shepherd and father he did not fail to visit almost daily the widows and virgins in the community, teaching and making steadfast their souls.

On the seventh day, he went to Sanaxar Monastery. The treasurer travelled two miles from the monastery to meet him, and at the ferry station on

Metropolitan Gabriel of Novgorod and St. Petersburg.

the Moksha River the entire Sanaxar brotherhood went out to meet him. From here, after receiving a blessing from him, they all walked together to the monastery. Having entered the church, they venerated the holy icons in the usual manner. Fr. Theodore rejoiced spiritually, praising the brethren for preserving their love for him and for completing the construction of the monastery church without him. Being unspeakably consoled and reconciled because of his arrival, they all began to live again in joyful calm of spirit.

21. PERSECUTION ANEW

The peace continued for only a short time. For it is not God's good pleasure that those whom He loves should live in ease while they are in the flesh. He wishes them rather to abide in afflictions, indignities, and insults. For by this are the sons of God set apart from the rest of mankind: that they live in afflictions.* On October 29, 1783, literally within several days after Fr. Theodore's return to Sanaxar Monastery after an absence of nine years, Hierodeacon Hilarion, who had been at one time with Elder Theodore at Solovki, brought slander against him in front of the entire brotherhood. Fr. Hilarion called the Elder "an adversary of the Church, a heretic and an atheist." The matter was addressed to the Synod, and after careful review they resolved that Hilarion be acknowledged as a slanderer and punished with all severity, at which he begged forgiveness of Fr. Theodore in front of the entire brotherhood.

Soon Benedict, the Superior of the Monastery, began to consider himself to have been debased, feeling that everyone who came to the monastery was circumventing him as the Superior and going to Fr. Theodore for instruction and conversation. Likewise, since many of the brethren began to go to Fr. Theodore to unburden their conscience, he was grieved thereby and out of dissatisfaction began to direct complaints against the Elder to the diocesan bishop. He stated that Fr. Theodore's disciples came to him in crowds and caused disturbance in the monastery regardless of the time of day and, moreover, without regard to the Superior's counsels.

Ascetical Homilies of St. Isaac the Syrian (Brookline: Holy Transfiguration Monastery, 1984), Homily 60, p. 293.

For this reason, investigators were sent. They named Fr. Theodore and his disciples accomplices merely on rumor and appearances, without questioning anyone—which might have revealed what was amiss in their company—probably because it would have been impossible to find anything blameworthy since it consisted solely of daily spiritual discourses. Fr. Theodore's teaching was offensive to Fr. Benedict because he often spoke of the passion of drunkenness as the fundamental cause of every disorder in monasteries, and of boasting as something unbecoming to the monastic calling, in place of which one must observe simplicity in one's activities and continence in one's life. As a consequence of this, access to Fr. Theodore was prohibited even for those with spiritual needs.

The cell-attendant of Metropolitan Gabriel, Archimandrite Theophan, reported this to His Eminence and asked him to compose a letter to Fr. Theodore, with the following content:

> Honorable Fr. Theodore, my beloved brother in Christ!
> I ask you, through your prayers, to help my life and the tasks related to my duties. I will always remain well-disposed toward you.
> Gabriel, Metropolitan of Novgorod and St. Petersburg

Learning of this, the Superior gave him a little freedom, seeing the good will of the Metropolitan toward Fr. Theodore. But then, he began anew to concoct unfair reports against him to the Bishop of Tambov. Again, Fr. Theodore was under house arrest—no one, either layman or monastic was allowed to go to him and speak about their spiritual needs. Only through letters did his disciples in Arzamas receive consolation in their afflictions and absolution of their conscience.

After the passage of several years, having instituted various restrictions against Fr. Theodore, the Superior, Hieromonk Benedict, fell ill. Fr. Theodore came to ask his forgiveness, but he, without saying a word, turned away toward the wall. Fr. Theodore left him thus. After his departure the Superior began to look around hither and thither, saying, "Why are people crowding into the cell?" Having suffered a little, he died on December 27, 1778.

22. REPOSE (†1791)

After the Superior's death, Fr. Theodore, having received freedom from the attacks and oppressive measures, travelled to Arzamas to address the spiritual needs of his flock. Arriving as accustomed at the Alexeyevsky Convent and speaking unexpectedly—in a manner contrary to his usual way—with special contrition and tears he explained in detail, among other things, the words of Psalm 136, *By the waters of Babylon...*, saying, "When the sons of Israel were deprived of Jerusalem, their fatherland, and could not see for themselves how they might find even the smallest consolation as sojourners in a foreign land, by the waters of Babylon, they sat down and wept. By means of such lamentation they offered an image of the state of all who live in misfortune upon the earth. We, too, must keep in our thoughts that in the impoverished life, like unto sojourners ever oppressed by misfortunes from their enemies, we will only find consolation for ourselves when we remember the Sion on high—*I remembered God and I was gladdened...* (Ps. 76:4)." When he spoke with contrition in this way, everyone wept—the Abbess and the sisters.

Then the Elder began to make haste to return to his Sanaxar Monastery. Having parted with everyone and given his blessing, he left Arzamas. On the road he travelled to Sarov Monastery, lovingly asked forgiveness of everyone, and hastened to Sanaxar. After his arrival, on Wednesday of Cheese-fare Week, his disciples gathered at noon in his cell. He spoke to all of them briefly in common and dismissed them to their cells. Two disciples from the nobility who lived in the monastery remained in his cell for their spiritual needs, but Fr. Theodore's countenance began to change. In the presence of the two disciples, he wept bitterly for about a quarter of an hour, saying how much he had sinned in his youth. Finally, he ordered them to go to their cells, saying that he was growing very weak.

For a long time it had not been uncommon for him to suffer from an internal illness, but this time everyone felt that this lack of strength was unusual. They left in grief. Not long after all had left, his cell-attendant came and—having offered the customary prayer three times, yet hearing no reply—entered without his blessing and saw Fr. Theodore reclining on his bed, praying. He immediately left and told the brethren about this. They all came together to see him in the evening but he would no longer say anything. Thus five hours transpired. At nine in the evening, his soul separated from his body into eternal life, on February 19, 1791. His body, although it lay in his warm room until his burial, did not give off the odor of death.

A slate gravestone was laid over the grave of the righteous Elder Theodore with the following inscription:

"Here is buried the 73-year-old Elder Hieromonk Theodore, having the surname Ushakov, the restorer of the Sanaxar Monastery, who was tonsured in the St. Alexander Nevsky Lavra, and who continued in the monastic life for forty-five years; in all respects a true Christian and a good monk. He reposed on February 19, 1791."* He was buried honorably in his own monastery.

23. HEAVENLY GLORY

Three months after his repose, Fr. Theodore appeared in a dream to his disciple, Archimandrite Ignatius of the Tikhvin Monastery. He wrote about this as follows, in order to inform the Alexeyevsky sisters in Arzamas.

"I was in a very serious illness and was already hopeless," he said. "In this condition, by God's authority, I saw my Elder, Fr. Theodore, in great glory in a vision during sleep. He showed me his monastery and many wonderful cells, each cell larger than your Alexeyevsky Convent. In them, I saw many of the Sanaxar monks and novices, your nuns and novices whom I had known who had departed from this life in complete rest, and many other people. Concerning others, my Elder said to me, 'And here are the Petersburg ones whom you didn't know.' Then he added, 'It's time for you to go to the monastery. Go.' Then, I woke up."

Fr. Archimandrite Ignatius reposed in the Simonov Monastery in 1796, on August 3, at ten in the evening on Sunday, just five years after his great Elder.

---

* *Life of Our Holy Father St. Theodore of Sanaxar* (Sanaxar Monastery, 1999), p.57.

24. NOTES OF HIS DISCIPLES

Archimandrite Theophan (Sokolov) of St. Cyril of New Lake Monastery left some precise notes about the dispersal of the monks of the Sanaxar Monastery.* These notes breathe a wonderful air of warmth and dedication. Here are some of them:

"Before departing [in banishment to Solovki], Fr. Theodore said to his brethren, especially to those not yet tonsured, 'Whoever wishes to live in the monastery, let him remain in it. Whoever does not so wish, let him depart with a blessing to wherever he wishes to go.' With such permission many left.

"I went to the Ostrovsky Hermitage of the Entrance of the Theotokos into the Temple, which lies about fifty-five miles from Moscow, to see the Elder Cleopas (a disciple of Blessed Paisius Velichkovsky). Novice Matthew, who was tonsured with the name Macarius and later became an Archimandrite in Peshnosha Monastery (I had lived in the same cell with him in the Sanaxar Monastery), went together with me. Then Fr. Ignatius left the Sanaxar Monastery. Afterwards, he was in the Florishchev Hermitage and after his ordination as hieromonk he became the treasurer. This father, in his departure from the Florishchev Hermitage to Petersburg, travelled by way of the Hermitage of the Entrance to see the Elder, Fr. Cleopas. The Elder placed an archimandrite's cross upon him. Stunned at this, Fr. Ignatius asked, 'Why have you placed upon me this archimandrite's cross, Batiushka?' The Elder said, 'After me you will become the Superior. And in another location you will be an archimandrite.'

"This came to pass in a short time. Returning from Petersburg, Fr. Ignatius came again to the Hermitage of the Entrance but did not find Fr. Cleopas still among the living. The brethren began to ask Fr. Ignatius to be their Superior and at their request he was made the Superior. Then, since Peshnosha Monastery (in which the relics of St. Methodius reposed) began to fall into total decline, Bishop Theophylactus of Pereyaslavl-Zaleski, wishing

---

*Published in the journal *Strannik* (St. Petersburg, 1862).

Archimandrite Macarius of Peshnosha Monastery,
pictured with the staff of St. Paisius Velichkovsky.

to revive the monastery, asked Fr. Ignatius to move there. Fr. Ignatius came
together with Fr. Macarius (who became Archimandrite after Fr. Ignatius).
When Fr. Ignatius was conscripted to be the Archimandrite in the Tikhvin
Monastery, he first wore the cross which Fr. Cleopas had placed upon him after his elevation as Archimandrite.

"I left the Hermitage of the Entrance of the Theotokos before Fathers
Ignatius and Macarius and, travelling with two monks—Anthony and Arsenius, who had come there from Moldavia—went to Tismana Monastery* in

---

*Founded in 1377 by St. Nicodemus of Tismana after the model of the monasteries of
Mount Athos, it became the center of spiritual enlightenment for all of the land of Romania.

Moldavia–Wallachia, where I was tonsured. But, by the unfathomable Providence of God, I came to the St. Alexander Nevsky Lavra in St. Petersburg. After our entire monastery moved from Moldavia to the Sophroniev Hermitage,* five men, among whom I was numbered, were requested to come to the Lavra from the Hermitage. We were all assigned certain responsibilities, and I was taken to serve as the cell-attendant of His Eminence (Metropolitan Gabriel). Here I had the opportunity to inform His Eminence about our Fr. Theodore, that he was not guilty of anything of which he had been accused. Therefore, he was returned once again to live at the Sanaxar Monastery by Imperial edict.

"I further consider it necessary to describe the manner in which Fr. Ignatius was elevated as Archimandrite. His Eminence Metropolitan Gabriel once visited the Tikhvin Monastery. As his cell-attendant, I went there with him. Inspecting the monastery he found it in great disrepair. The Archimandrite at the time was a certain Elder Euthymius. Returning from this monastery to Petersburg, His Eminence asked me, 'Who should I appoint to be Archimandrite in Tikhvin?'

"I replied, 'If you please, Your Eminence, the Abbot of Peshnosha, Ignatius.'

"He asked me, 'Do you know him?'

"I said that we had lived together in the Sanaxar Monastery. Then he directed a report to be written to the Synod which he took with him, suggesting to the Synod that the Tikhvin Monastery needed to be repaired as he had personally seen it in great ruin. He added that he found Abbot Ignatius of Pesnosha capable of this task. But, since Fr. Ignatius had not studied theology or the other higher sciences—although he was endowed with great natural gifts—the Synod could not consent to elevate this unlettered man as an Archimandrite. For this reason the matter was prolonged for half a year. In the end, returning from the Synod, His Eminence Metropolitan Gabriel joyfully exclaimed, 'Glory be to God, the Synod has agreed!'

"In such a manner Fr. Ignatius was elevated as Archimandrite. He

---

*On account of the approach of the occupation of Wallachia by Turkish troops, Archimandrite Theodosius and his brotherhood elected to move to Russia to avoid reprisals for their sympathies with the Russian Army.

Archimandrite Theophan of New Lake Monastery.

introduced order into the Tikhvin Monastery. He began the painting of the wall frescoes in the Tikhvin Catholicon. Then Fr. Archimandrite Ignatius was transferred to the Moscow Simonov Monastery which had been closed and had fallen to such degradation that a cavalry regiment was boarded there. He renewed it with the care and material aid of the eminent Muscovite citizen Athanasius Ivanovich Dolgov (who, here in the New Lake Monastery, was so generous as to make an iconostasis in the Catholicon). By his help and that of a pious and eminent citizen, Simeon Prokofievich Vasiliev, a gilded silver reliquary [for the founder of the St. Cyril of New Lake

Monastery] was made in 1795, two years after my entrance into the [New Lake] monastery."

25. THREE NOVICES WHO DISOBEYED ELDER THEODORE
(From the Notes of Archimandrite Theophan)

"Of the three novices mentioned above who did not obey Fr. Theodore's exhortation, but went of their own will into the desert, considering the desert life more congenial to fasting, prayer and hesychasm, one was Peter Borisovich, formerly a lieutenant. Leaving Sanaxar for the woods, he lived in solitude for three years.* Then, not having a counselor, he foolishly took the Lord's words: *If thy right hand offend thee cut it off* (Matt. 5:30), in a mistaken sense, and wanting to show his fulfillment of these words in reality, in a way that no one up to that time had ever carried them out, he cut off his left hand completely. The blood poured out terribly and his life was in danger. But someone unseen (obviously an angel of God) asked him sternly, 'What brazen thing have you done? Bind the wound or you'll die.' He bound it right away and then felt no more pain. Fr. Nazarius, formerly of Sarov Monastery and then the Abbot of Valaam Monastery, hearing about this, came straight from Valaam to the sick man in the woods and took him with him to Valaam. There he was tonsured with the name Paul and, after living a while longer, died.**

"Abbot Nazarius, after being released from the governance of the Valaam Monastery, moved back again from Valaam to Sarov Monastery. There, in reclusion near Sarov Monastery, he died and was buried in the monastery.

"The second novice, Basil Ivanovich Makarov, also a former lieutenant, having left Sanaxar, did not even go to the woods but came to Moscow. At his own request he was accepted into the Novo-Spassky Monastery. Having lived there a certain time, he prepared for monastic tonsure. A decree was even

---

*This incident probably took place before 1774 when Elder Nazarius was still in Sarov, since in 1783, when Fr. Theodore returned to Sanaxar, he was no longer Abbot and would not have been able to create such a striking scene in the refectory. It is most likely that after this event happened, Peter went astray and so was taken under the "wing" of Elder Nazarius who then took him to Valaam with him when he left Sarov in 1781.

**See a similar account with different details in "The Life of the Monk and Desert-dweller Basilisk," *The Sayings of the Schemamonk Zosima* (Moscow, 1863), pp. 77–81.

received allowing his tonsure when he, preparing for this and cleaning his cell, found a stocking with money behind his stove in some rubbish. His thoughts wavered and he refused to be tonsured. One nobleman, who would come to him for spiritual benefit, came to the monastery to witness his tonsure. Novice Basil told him that now he didn't intend to receive the tonsure but wanted to still live a while longer in the world. That nobleman, being single, began to entreat him to live in his house which was located in Moscow in the parish of the Great Martyr Nicetas, on Vshiva hill behind the Yauza river. Basil agreed and, refusing the tonsure, moved to his house. Even more to his liking, a church was near and services were celebrated daily.

"After a certain time, the nobleman began to ask him to take a little trip to Petersburg and make the effort to get his rank back. Basil agreed. The officer dressed him in a fine officer's outfit and bestowed on him some money. Arriving in Petersburg, he found a secluded apartment which suited his good disposition for a quiet life. There in that apartment, in another suite, there were living a widow and her daughter. Learning after a certain time that he was meek and behaved humbly, and that he was a bachelor, the widow began to suggest that he agree to marry her daughter. He, having forgotten Fr. Theodore's prophecy, married this virgin and, after finishing the affairs entrusted to him, dismissed the servant given him by the nobleman and settled on a plot of land belonging to his mother-in-law in the Tikhvin region. He lived here for some time until his wife died, at which point he again left secular life and entered the Tikhvin Monastery. This was while Archimandrite Ignatius was there, with whom he had lived in Sanaxar. Here, Basil was tonsured with the name Vitaly. As an altar-assistant, he monitored the candles in the Catholicon on the left side and so reposed.

"The third novice was Alexis Andreyevich from the town of Kineshma. What his father did is not known, but it was heard that they lived with sufficient means. Alexis, leaving the monastery, came to his father's house and began to ask him to build him a cell in the garden for a life of seclusion. His father fulfilled his wish eagerly and Alexis started to live as a recluse. But inasmuch as he did not have an instructor, he took it upon himself to fast according to his own understanding, and went to such an extreme that he no longer knew who he was. The Old-Believers, learning of his life, began to come to him and to lure him into their sect and actually accomplished this. Then they tonsured him and clothed him according to the Old-Ritualist practice. His father left him to himself. But it seems that God remembered the labors that he endured and did not allow him to die in delusion. One novice of the Sanaxar Monastery from the merchant class, Philip Philipovich, who lived at that time in the Florishchev Hermitage, learned about Novice Alexis, with whom he had lived together in Sanaxar, and wanted to visit him. He came to his parent's house in the city of Kineshma and asked about Alexis, begging his father to let him see him. Having come to him, he saw him in utter languor, clothed like a sectarian, and asked him, 'Do you know me?' Glancing at him, he said, 'You are Philip Philipovich.' Philip said to him, 'You've been led astray by the Old-Believers. Look, your life has already come to an end. Turn to the Holy Church, confess and partake of the Holy Mysteries.' Though he claimed that the Old-Believers had taught him the truth, Philip nevertheless proved to him that they themselves had gone astray and had led others into ruin. Finally, with God's help, he brought him to his senses. They called a priest who, having confessed him and given him the Holy Mysteries, gave him hope in God's mercy. Afterwards, Alexis soon reposed and was buried in the church by the novice Philip."

II

Spiritual Counsels
of Elder Theodore

ВИДЪ САНАКСАРСКАГО БОГОРОДИЦКАГО ОБЩЕЖИТЕЛЬНАГО МОНАСТЫРЯ СЪ ЮГО-ЗАПАДНОЙ СТОРОНЫ.

ИЗДАНІЕ ТАМБОВСКОЙ ГУБЕРНІИ, ГОРОДА ТЕМНИКОВА, СТРОИТЕЛЯ ІЕРОМОНАХА АВГУСТИНА СЪ БРАТІЕЮ.

Отъ Московскаго Духовно-Цензурнаго Комитета печать дозволяется Москва Октября 19 дня 1888 года. Цензоръ священникъ Александръ Гиляревскій

View of the Sanaxar Monastery of the Theotokos from the southwest.

CHAPTER ONE

*Short Instructions of Elder Theodore**

1. ON MAN

Question: I wish to understand—for what purpose did God create man to dwell upon the earth?

Answer: God created man to dwell upon the earth unto eternal and unending life, unto the adoption of sonship and the inheritance of His Divine Kingdom. For this reason we call God Father, saying: "Our Father, who art in Heaven," and again, in the words of the Gospel of John the Theologian: *As many as received Him, to them gave He power to become the sons of God, to them that believe on His name* (John 1:12). Hear the Savior Christ Himself, who says to the Father: *O holy Father! Keep through Thine own name those whom Thou hast given Me, that they may be one, as We are* (John 17:11), that is, that they also may be together with Us. And again the word of the Gospel spoken by the Lord: *Come, ye blessed of My Father, inherit the kingdom prepared for you from the foundation of the world* (Matt. 25:34).

Question: If God created man to this purpose, that he might become a son of God and an heir of His Kingdom, then why did He separate him from Himself to dwell upon the earth in such weak flesh?

---

*Published in "The Life of Fr. Theodore, the Former Abbot of Sanaxar Monastery" (Moscow, University Press, 1847), p. 42ff. Two notebooks containing more of Elder Theodore's teachings were written down by the novice Ivan Evdokimovich, who at the monastic tonsure was named Ioannicius. (He was subsequently the Abbot of Konevets Monastery, where he was later replaced; he requested to retire to the Sarov Monastery where he eventually reposed.) Having written down these teachings, Novice Ivan brought them to Elder Theodore for review and approval. Leaving the monastery, Novice Ivan wanted to take these teachings with him, but they were taken from him by several of his adversaries who burnt them and thereby deprived many of much good by which they might have profited to the salvation of their souls.

Answer: As God so loved man whom He had created for adoption unto sonship and to receive the eternal inheritance of His Kingdom—so, too, did God wish that man might show his love for God. For this He endowed him with corruptible and infirm flesh and placed him to dwell upon the earth, and gave him a Divine commandment and enjoined him to battle with the enemy, that beholding his labors and obedience to his Creator, God would know the love of men toward Himself.

2. CONCERNING WARFARE WITH THE ENEMY

Question: With which enemy did God command man to do battle?

Answer: The Holy Spirit says in the Apocalypse: *To him that overcometh will I grant to sit with Me in My throne* (Rev. 3:21). But whom is man commanded to overcome? Concerning this listen to Christ the Savior Himself, the first Victor. For to this end did He come down to earth and take flesh like our flesh, that He might show us a model of His labors and love for the Father, by His victory over the enemy. Listen to what He says to His disciples, and as well to all men: *In the world ye shall have tribulation, but be of good cheer; I have overcome the world* (John 16:33). By these words of Christ we should understand that together with the world, the world-lover—the devil—is also overcome. For there is warfare at all times with him, concerning which the Apostle speaks: *For we wrestle not against flesh and blood, but against principalities, against powers, against the rulers of the darkness of this world, against spiritual wickedness in the underheaven* (Eph. 6:12). In other parts of the Scriptures the enemy, the devil, is called the prince of this world (cf. John 12:31)—a prince not of created things, but of the passionate lovers of created things. He has the authority to deceive by the passions and to pierce the slothful and men insensitive to the love of God with love for the passions. The three chief passions which the devil loves above all others are vainglory, avarice and licentiousness; by these three passions the enemy has lured man into transgressing all the commandments of God. He has incited much enmity, has spawned the spilling of blood, led others into many other sinful passions, and transformed love for God and neighbor into enmity, according to the Apostle's word: *Whosoever will be a friend of the world is the enemy of*

God (James 4:4). By means of these passions this maliciously cunning enemy also addressed Christ the Savior Himself, but he was vanquished and cast down—not only by Christ's continence, but also by His very outpoured Blood and death on the Cross. The enemy, the devil, likewise takes up arms against the entire human race by means of these passions, and overcomes the slothful and those negligent of God's love. He knows that man is beloved of God and for this reason is to dwell on the earth that he might keep His ordinances, and through this to demonstrate his love for God. For this reason the enemy strives to deceive man into transgressing the Lord's commandments and thereby to separate man from God's love. For this cause a war with him lies before us—to lay low the devil, that is, to mortify one's passions and not to become his obedient servants, not only by simply refraining from the allure of the passions, but also to abide in patience for the sake of God's righteousness, even unto death. Let such be our warfare against him, and may such a victory be accomplished. For this have we been sent by God to live for a while upon the earth—that through such a life of trial we may come to know perfectly the love of God in us and thereby become sons of God and be made heirs of His Kingdom, if we do not voluntarily deprive ourselves of this inheritance by the passions.

If someone were to say that man was created by God that he might be in Paradise, but he sinned of his own free will and for this was cast out of Paradise, and not that God placed him on the earth, requiring love from him, we would reply to this as previously: that God, before He had created man, knew that man whom He would create would sin—that is, that he would not keep His commandments and would be cast out of Paradise to live upon the earth. This too did God know—that He would send His Son, our Lord Jesus Christ, the Savior of the entire human race for those who have faith in Him as our Savior, to redeem the ancestral sin, and that through this the gates of God's Kingdom would be opened again unto man.

For this reason God did not hinder the sin of the first man whom He had created for eternal life. Likewise, the expulsion of man from Paradise, by God's prescience and dispensation, was like an exile—that man would live on the earth and toil, that is, war with the adversary, the devil, according to the words of the Apostle: *We wrestle not against flesh and blood, but against principalities, against powers, against the rulers of the darkness of this world, against spiritual wickedness in the underheaven* (Eph. 6:12). Man is to war with the devil through the fulfilling of God's ordinances and His holy commandments, given us by Christ our Savior, in the unity of His Divine Love, according to the word of the Lord: *If a man love me, he will keep my words: ... He that loveth me not keepeth not my sayings* (John 14:23-24). According to these words of the Lord, if a man loves his Lord, that is, if he keeps His sayings, living on the earth and engaging in combat with His enemy—the evil devil—and with all the passions, then God, seeing his labors ever increasing, will love him as His own son, as the Lord saith: *He that hath my commandments, and keepeth them, he it is that loveth Me: and he that loveth Me shall be loved by My Father, and I will love him, and will manifest Myself to him* (John 14:21). By these words the Lord God reckons us His sons and heirs of His Divine Kingdom.

Question: What else must man, an Orthodox Christian, do to inherit eternal life?

Answer: He must have right faith and virtues.

Question: What is faith?

Answer: Faith is the evidence of things not seen, when we believe while not seeing but only hearing from God's revelation.

Question: What are good works or virtues?

Answer: Good works or the virtues consist in the fulfillment of God's commandments.

Question: In what do the commandments of God consist?

Answer: The first commandment of God is to love God with all one's soul, more than anything, and more than one's own self.

Question: How may the love of God be known among men?

Answer: Love for God is known from the fulfilling of God's commandments, according to the Lord's word: *If a man loves Me, he will keep my commandments* (cf. John 14:21, 23).

Question: What other commandments originate from the love of God?

Answer: From the love of God there follows the second commandment of Christ—to love one's neighbor as one's self: on these two commandments, according to the word of the Lord, hang all the Law and the Prophets, that is, the whole Law and Prophets taught this.

3. ON VIRTUE AND SIN

Question: How am I to understand what is sin and what is virtue?

Answer: Virtue is the fulfilling of God's commandments, while sin is the transgression of these commandments.

Question: What are the fruits of the virtues?

Answer: The first fruit of virtue is scorn for the things of earth and joy toward the things of heaven, according to the Apostle who said: *Eye hath not seen, nor ear heard, neither have entered into the heart of man, the things which God hath prepared for those who love Him* (I Cor. 2:9). In the words of Christ concerning the Beatitudes there is indicated what is necessary in order to receive all the fruits of virtue. *Blessed are the poor in spirit,* that is, those who acknowledge their poverty, their lack of virtue. *Blessed are those who mourn,* that is, that for the sake of such poverty they might not be deprived of the Lord's mercy. Further He adds, *Blessed are the merciful, Blessed are the pure in heart, Blessed are the peacemakers, Blessed are they that are persecuted for righteousness' sake,* etc. (Matt. 5:3-10). And again Christ says: *Love your enemies ... do good to them that hate you* (Matt. 5:44). Again: *Learn of Me, for I am meek and lowly in heart* (Matt. 11:29). And again: *For I was an hungered and ye gave Me meat: I was thirsty, and ye gave Me drink: I was a stranger, and ye took Me in: naked, and ye clothed Me: I was sick and in prison, and ye came unto Me* (Matt 25:35-36). Paul, the divine Apostle, adds to this these fruits: *The fruit of the Spirit is love, joy, peace, long-suffering, goodness, gentleness, faith, meekness, temperance.... And they that are Christ's have crucified the flesh with the affections and lusts* (Gal. 5:22,24), and by this he sets forth the crucifixion of the love of this world which is central to those who live the monastic life.

Question: What constitute the fruits of sin?

Answer: The fruits of sin are these: first, a persistently lascivious and world-loving life about which the holy Apostle James speaks clearly: *Ye adulterers and adulteresses, know ye not that the friendship of the world is enmity with God? Whosoever therefore will be a friend of the world is the enemy of God* (James 4:4). What the Apostle calls "the world" is voluptuous, unrelenting human love (predilection), love of riches, of human glory or luxury, as well as a lukewarm, leisurely and flesh-pleasing life. And again the holy Apostle Paul calls the sensuous human life fleshly wisdom: *The carnal mind is in enmity against God, for it is not subject to the law of God, neither indeed can be* (Rom. 8:7), as long as man persists in such a licentious life. Passion is constant reprehensible love for any object. The lovers of the world wallow in the first three soul-destroying passions—in vainglory, in avarice and in licentiousness—for from these three passions, as from three great springs, many other founts of sin flow forth—for example, offense to one's neighbor, envy, hatred, remembrance of evil, wrath, pride, lying, slander, reproach, derision, cheating, stealing, stinginess, unkindness, unrighteous man-pleasing and collaboration, banqueting with disorderly people, drunkenness, fornication, swearing, blasphemy and every other sinful impure action, which the Savior Christ indicates, saying: *Every idle word that men shall speak, they shall give account thereof in the day of judgment* (Matt. 12:36). And further: *Woe unto you that laugh now, for ye shall mourn and weep* (Luke 6:25). Again: *Take heed to yourselves, lest at any time your hearts be overcharged with surfeiting, and drunkenness and cares of this life,* that is, with the passionate lusts, *and that day* of judgment *come upon you unawares* (Luke 21:34). Again the holy Apostle Paul writes: *Let no corrupt communication proceed out of your mouth* (Eph. 4:29). *Grieve not the Holy Spirit of God, whereby ye are sealed unto the day of redemption* (Eph. 4:30). That which was said concerning a corrupt communication pertains also to an idle word, or those that are blasphemous or evoke laughter. Again, the same Apostle says: *Mortify therefore your members which are upon the earth: fornication, uncleanness, inordinate affection, evil concupiscence and covetousness, which is idolatry: for which things' sake the wrath of God cometh on the children of disobedience* (Col. 3:5-6).

In fulfilling the commandments of God and in overcoming the devil and the soul-destroying passions we should have constant remembrance of God and prayer so as to receive the Lord's help, through which we might be able to stand against all the devil's snares.

4. WHAT IS PLEASING TO GOD AND WHAT IS CONTRARY TO HIM?

One who wishes to receive the mercy of God must keep God's commandments. God's commandments enjoin us to do virtuous deeds and to refrain from evil works.

In order to please God it is necessary to entreat Him with a contrite heart that He might forgive us our sins and mercifully order our life unto salvation, and to thank Him for all His mercies, to attend the Church of God on every feast, to listen in everything to what the Holy Church ordains, while on other days to labor without slothfulness at whatever task one has, to give alms to the poor from one's own labors and to bring offerings to God's Church, and to help one another in their needs. Whoever has enmity toward someone must forgive him without harboring anger. Everyone who finds himself in misfortune, disaster or some other necessity through no fault of his own must bear it nobly without grieving, but with thanksgiving to God. One must always have in remembrance the fear of God so as to be delivered from eternal torment, and must always beseech God that He might grant us to be in the Heavenly Kingdom. All this is pleasing to God.

In order to refrain from the works of evil, one must not offend another, not steal what belongs to someone else, neither appropriate anything by deceit; neither lie, nor quarrel with one another, become angry, remember evil; neither live like a prodigal, like a drunkard, nor instigate laughter, swear or speak idly, nor act like a buffoon or a dancer; neither practice magic or other works of the unclean spirits, nor turn in times of illness to sorcerers or those who cast spells. All this is in opposition to God.

5. ON THE MONASTIC LIFE

The Elder's question: Why, brother, have you left the world and come to the monastery?

Answer of the one who has come: For the surest means of the salvation of my soul, honorable father!

Question of the seeker: I pray, honorable father, make known to me what my stay in the monastery requires for my salvation.

Answer: One's stay in the monastery requires one to live a monastic life.

Question: But what is a monk and how should he live?

Answer: A monk is a man who is separated from the world and from all desires that are in the world, that is, from father, mother, wife, children, friends and relatives, from riches and from all human glory, for he must devote all his love to the One God alone, according to the Apostle's words: *I count all things but dung, that I may win Christ* (cf. Phil. 3:8). And again: *The world is crucified unto me, and I unto the world* (Gal. 6:14), that is, the world takes no delight in me as one dead, nor do I rejoice in the world, for I am dead. Under such a condition is a monk to be understood and such must he be.

Question: I beseech you to further explain to me—what else does such a monk need for salvation?

Answer: He should be non-acquisitive in regard to property and poverty; second, he should have purity of body and soul; and third, obedience.

6. CONCERNING MONASTIC POVERTY

Question: Is it only in regard to possessions that a monk is to exercise poverty?

Answer: Poverty is to be understood in two ways. Material poverty is one thing; another is spiritual poverty, that is, the knowledge of our unworthiness before God, our baseness and lack of the riches of virtue, of the fact that we are perishing because of our laziness. Monks who are conscious of their own spiritual poverty must sorrow each day, so that for the sake of this poverty they are not deprived of the mercies of the Lord. Christ extols the lowly of spirit: *Blessed are the poor in spirit, for theirs is the Kingdom of Heaven. Blessed are they that mourn, for they shall be comforted* (Matt. 5:3-4).

7. ON PURITY OF SOUL AND BODY

Question: What is purity of body and soul?

Answer: Bodily purity consists in preserving oneself from every kind of carnal union or fornication. Spiritual purity is that purity whereby one is preserved in one's soul from every lascivious sin; for the soul which persisteth in sins is defiled and impure and in truth is called in Scripture a whore and an adulteress because it has fallen away from its love for Christ its Bridegroom, and has given itself over to the soul-destroying passions and above all, through the passions, to the devil himself, for he is the prince of such passions. Thus the soul becomes the bride of satan, because it has given its love to him. To be pure from sin means not only to preserve oneself from sinful acts, but not even to be attracted to them in thought, according to the Lord's word: *Blessed are the pure in heart, for they shall see God* (Matt 5:8).

8. ON OBEDIENCE

Question: What is obedience?

Answer: Obedience is cutting off one's will and submitting oneself, in everything lawful and not harmful to the soul, to the Abbot as well as to all the brethren, and carrying out whatever one might be commanded, as long as it is not harmful to the soul.

Question: After these things, what other necessary virtues lead a monk to salvation?

Answer: After these follow humility, patience and continence.

9. CONCERNING HUMILITY

Question: What is humility?

Answer: Humility is to think nothing great or exalted about oneself both before God and before men. Before God, because one is always a sinner, for even if he does do something good, he must know that he did it not of himself, but solely by the Lord's help, according to the words of the Apostle: *Not that we are sufficient of ourselves to think any thing as of ourselves, but our sufficiency is of God* (II Cor. 3:5). For this reason think nothing highly about yourself, but above all remember the words of the Prophet: *I am a worm* before God, *and not a man, a reproach of men and the outcast of the people* (Ps. 21:6). Consider yourself the least before men and, living in the brotherhood, prefer to have the least in everything, choose the lowest place, be first to bow to a brother, love the meanest clothes, attend to every necessary task without murmuring, and preserve silence. If it is necessary to say something, do not speak obstinately but meekly and humbly make yourself to be heard. When you are upbraided or endure vexation from others, do not grow angry and think only that you are the least of all and the servant of all—this is perfect humility.

10. ON PATIENCE

Question: What is patience?

Answer: Patience consists in not desponding or grieving in any difficult circumstances, whether in bodily labors or amidst thoughts of the soul, but manfully and good-naturedly enduring all suffering of afflictions, even until death, with hope in God's loving-kindness, according to the Lord's word: *Come unto Me, all ye who labor and are heavy laden, and I will give you rest* (Matt 11:28). And again: *He that endureth to the end,* He says, *shall be saved* (Matt. 10:22).

11. ON CONTINENCE

Question: What is continence?

Answer: Continence is the restraint of excessive lusts, beyond what is necessary, toward everything, according to the Apostle's word: *Make not provision for the flesh, to fulfill the lusts thereof* (Rom. 13:14). Continence is necessary in various circumstances: in relation to the belly, the tongue, the sight, the hearing, and to every mental passion of the flesh or spirit. Continence of the stomach consists in abstaining from excess of delicious foods and from eating at improper times; even if the desire moves one to do so, do not allow it to be carried out and restrain yourself in every way. The tongue is eagerly moved by idle talking, blasphemy and many other unseemly things, but again do not allow this and restrain it in every way possible. The sight stretches its gaze towards various unlawful deeds and to seductive amusements and these also should not be allowed and should be restrained. The hearing desires to listen to idle conversations and jesting or to demonic songs and one should not permit the ears to hear such things and should refrain in every way from listening to them. One should not allow oneself to fulfill any excessive desires, beyond what is necessary, and should refrain from them. This is continence.

12. ON PRAYER

Question: What else is needed for the fulfillment of the aforementioned virtues?

Answer: To perform the aforementioned virtues there is still needed prayer to God, by which all of this will become possible to carry out, according to the Lord's word: *Without Me ye can do nothing* (John 15:5). For this reason every man, but above all the monk, should persevere in unceasing prayer, according to the Apostle's word: *Pray unceasingly* (I Thes. 5:17). *Be vigilant* (pray always); *because your adversary the devil, as a roaring lion, walketh about, seeking whom he may devour* (I Peter 5:8). For this reason the Lord said: *Watch ye and pray, lest ye enter into temptation* (Mark 14:38). Enjoining us to conduct unceasing prayer, the Divine Apostle signifies noetic, not merely rational prayer—for prayer is twofold: one aspect is rational, the other is noetic. Rational prayer is temporary prayer, as much as and for as long as one desires. Noetic [or mental] prayer can be offered at any time, according to the Apostle's word: *Whether ye eat, or drink, or whatsoever ye do, do all to the glory of God* (I Cor. 10:31); that is, remember the Lord your God at all times. How is noetic prayer to be understood? Noetic prayer is such that a man, but especially a monk, ever lifts his mind to God and asks His Divine aid in victory over our adversary and over the soul-destroying passions and in the fulfillment of the virtues.

13. MORE ON PRAYER AND THE VIRTUES

Being in prayer or at his tasks, a monk must always say to himself: "Let us lift up our heart," and take extreme care that no manner of weakness might diminish his spiritual fervency toward God or virtue.

While taking food in the refectory with one's lips, one is to take in the word of God [which is always read during the meals in monasteries] with one's ears. If he happens to be offered meager and unappetizing food, he must rejoice and be consoled even more, that the meal itself has given him an opportunity to celebrate his victory over the passions.

In conversation one should be meek, not prone to laughter, wise, of few words, and should never let words issue forth from his lips without thinking. With laymen one should not talk about anything other than what is necessary for their instruction in the virtues.

A monk must not be affectionate towards anyone or in anything nor should he pretend to be learned or holy. Therefore he should reply meekly and, in the case of conversations about books, he should listen but not speak. When he is forced to speak he should not take care about oratorical beauty but let his speech be simple and even coarse rather than embellished.

Let all things done in common—that is, prayer, obediences, and the reading of books—be performed not out of habit but from a warm disposition and fervor toward God.

Let common prayers be preferred above private prayers, for common prayer is the image of the future heavenly glory. For this reason it befits a monk not to be slothful in common prayer, but zealous, as a good soldier of Christ.

Upon encountering people do not show yourself to be despondent and at the same time do not tell blasphemous jokes; let your laughter be only a grin full of meekness and chastity.

14. ON THE WORDS: "PAY HEED TO YOURSELF"

Pay heed to yourself—he who attends to himself will not meddle in the affairs of others in an untimely, shameless or curious way. Pay heed to yourself—a disorderly, lustful or evil eye sees not its own falls but those of others. It does not notice its own sins but beholds the faults of others in a way that is exceedingly clear; it does not even want to know of its own affairs but finds fault with those of others; it is cool toward its own guilt but flares up at the errors of others. In short, as the Lord has said, such an eye sees not the beam that is in itself, but sees the splinter in that of another (cf. Matt. 7:3).

A brother, when he offends another brother, is as if in delirium. When he sins against his neighbor he has taken leave of his senses; he knows not himself and is a stranger to the love of mankind. If someone will not co-suffer with his brother or come to his aid, if he will not treat him with patience, nor heal him by means of forgiveness, he is himself not healthy; he is ailing and infirm. Such a one does not have compassion.

Let a man think of himself as a sinner and hate vengeance. You will sin tomorrow against him who has sinned against you now. He will be your judge who previously was guilty before you, and he will grant you forgiveness, if you have granted it to him. But if you did not forgive him, then he will either not grant you forgiveness or, if he does grant it, he will regard his forgiveness to be more valuable than it really is. Absolve the sinner and forgive the one who repents, so that when you sin, your compassion will be recompensed to you and not in vain. He who forgives others has been freed from torments, has anticipated the tribunal, has escaped the judgment, has prepared for himself forgiveness in advance before he sins.

Let us submit to Christ and with all the power of love bear the vilification, beatings and the burdens of brothers who are malicious toward us, that we may deliver them from torment and may receive for ourselves the eternal reward for patience. Neither let the servant refuse to receive from his fellow-servants that which our Lord was pleased to receive from His servants (the Jews) for the sake of His servants (all those whom He redeemed). He turned not His face away from mockery, He ordered us to give to one who would take away our garment our cloak as well, to emulate willingly and voluntarily even until death the labors and suffering (for the race of mankind) which He took upon Himself out of His love. Therefore, brethren, if our Lord considered it a worthwhile undertaking to endure, how can it not be considered fitting for His servants to endure as well?

Why is it that we are sometimes not bored to stand for an entire day before men, but have we no desire to stand for a few minutes before God?

15. ON THE THREE ASPECTS OF THE SOUL

Let it be known: Those who are glorified in this world cannot fashion the fruits of heaven. Virtue that is displayed disappears.

The soul has three aspects within which require activity: the intelligent, appetitive and the incensive; and likewise, three outward members: the desire for glory, sweets and possessions. The soul that wisely examines the life of the Lord Jesus in the flesh sees that by the four chief virtues, that is, by wisdom, righteousness, chastity and courage, these two triads are mastered and healed by the grace of the Lord Jesus, and the mind is enlightened, being led up on high. By fasting Jesus Christ has mastered the appetitive part; by vigilance and silent prayer He has mastered the intelligent; and He has mastered the incensive by opposing it; for example: *If I have spoken evil, bear witness to the evil: but if well, why smitest thou me?* (John 18:23). When necessary, He did not speak in defiance (cf. Luke 23:9), and He prayed for those who abused Him. This is how the wrathful should behave: strike the devil by contradiction; when oppressed by man, and by those who are oppressed by satan, reply with silence and long-suffering, and offer prayer for them. Take note—the Lord, was spat upon, received abuse, and endured derision and cursing. This is the antidote for vainglory! He was given vinegar to drink, He was fed gall, and was pierced by a spear. This is the remedy for the delight in sweets! He was hung naked upon the Cross, abandoned and scorned by all, like some beggar or pauper. This is the prescription for abolishing avarice!

Chapter Two

Soul-profiting Counsels of Fr. Theodore
to his Disciples

1. REVELATION OF THOUGHTS*

The devil, seeing himself put to shame not only by the Elder [Epicte-
tus], but also by the youth [Astion], and filled with greed for the souls of
men, was torn with jealousy, and armed himself in every way by his craftiness
yet he had no success. But he found the following opportune moment against
the younger one: On a certain day Astion went out without the Elder's blessing to the river to draw water. The enemy, seeing that Astion was not pro-
tected by the Elder's blessing, perhaps by God's allowance, assailed him with
certain foul thoughts and troubled the youth's soul. Astion, returning to his
cell, was ashamed to confess these thoughts to his spiritual father, and was
conquered, fighting with them for three days. He fasted, prayed with tears
and exhausted his flesh with labors, but he could not in any way repel the unclean thoughts.

The Elder, seeing the youth troubled, said to him: "What has happened
child, for I behold you troubled in an unusual way? The grief which I see in
you, is not the grief of the saints who take pains over their salvation. It seems
to me that this sorrow of yours is a deadly sorrow like that through which Judas the betrayer perished."

Then Astion began to confess, saying: "Having conversed with you,
Father, in the presence of honorable men about the heavenly mysteries, I
was ashamed to ask a blessing of you in the presence of these men. I went
without your blessing for water and found myself on the way in a dark
cloud of filthy thoughts and it is now the third day that I cannot dispel

---

*Captions provided by the editors of the English edition.

89

LITTLE RUSSIAN PHILOKALIA

them from myself. The holy Elder, gazing threateningly at him, said: "Why have you gone outside the door of the cell without my command? Do you not know that a superior's blessing is an unassailable wall to the young, and mighty armor and an invincible weapon against the devil?" Having said this he commanded him to stretch himself out on the ground crosswise in prayer, stretching himself out as well, and together they both entreated God with tears. Having arisen from the earth after sufficient prayer, the blessed Astion beheld a certain black youth with a burning candle fleeing from him and saying: "Your confession shook my great powers today and your prayer has disarmed me."*

2. WAR WITH THE WORLD**

A certain youth sought to renounce the world, and having many times left the world for the monastery, thoughts came back to him speaking to him about worldly things, for he had been exceedingly rich. Leaving one day, he walked around and stirred up a lot of dust, for he would turn back again and again. He suddenly undressed, threw away his clothes and ran naked as fast as he could to the monastery. The Lord revealed this to a certain Elder, saying, "Arise and receive My sufferer."

3. SEPARATION FROM GOD

A priest said, "We do little at the few services, but the Lord reveals to us the mysteries, whereas you perform so many labors, vigils, fasts, stillness and say that God doesn't reveal anything to you. Why? Because you have evil thoughts in your hearts and this is what separates you from your God and why He does not tell you His mysteries." As the fathers heard, they marvelled saying, "For vile thoughts separate us from God."

---

*From the Lives of the Saints for the Seventh of July. See also, Ioanichie Balan, Archimandrite, *Romanian Patericon: Saints of the Romanian Orthodox Church, Vol. I* (Forestville, Calif.: St. Herman of Alaska Brotherhood, 1996), pp. 30–31.

**This and the following counsels in this chapter are from the *Skete Patericon* (the Lives of the Holy Fathers of Scetis).

4. WAR WITH THOUGHTS

Having sometimes seen a brother in the common life praying in his hut, behold, a demon came and stood in front of his hut. Because the brother was praying, he could not enter, but as soon as he stopped praying, the demon entered into his hut (that is, into his cell). One who entertains thoughts can not be continent.

5. SILENCE AS FEAR OF GOD

What is silence and what benefit is to be derived from it? One Elder said this: "Silence is to sit in one's cell with understanding and the fear of God, without having any opinion or high-mindedness. Such silence gives birth to all the virtues and preserves the monk from all the arrows of the enemy, not allowing him to be wounded by them."

6. REASONING CAUSES EVIL DISTRUST

How are we to live, father? The Elder said: "I have never known that I have told one of you to do something if I have not first practiced what I had considered: so do not grow angry with me. No one has caused dissensions of evil distrust in the Holy Church other than by one's own reasoning, and by not loving God and one another exceedingly."

7. DANGER OF WICKED THOUGHTS

Child, it is not a fast if you refrain from food and yet slander someone, judge someone, remember evil or accept wicked thoughts. It would be better if you would eat five helpings of food but keep yourself from these dangers. Do you not know that one can fulfill his every desire in thought without externally satiating himself with food and drink?

8. NOT BEING HEARD DUE TO LACK OF PRAYER

Restrain the young with all the authority of the Superior. For the demon of fornication presents us not only with idleness and sleep but also disturbs us with all other passions.

Inasmuch as glory and honor are promised to those who serve the Lord unceasingly, torment is prepared for those who approach the monastic task in sloth and carelessness. Woe unto you, as it is written, if you do not pray—for if you do not pray, you will not be heard.

9. RENUNCIATION OF THE WORLD

Denial of this world—do not presume that this is anything other than the Cross and death. Come to know what is the power of this crucifixion, since through it you will not live to anyone else, but He Who was crucified for you will live in you. In this manner, therefore, in which the Master was crucified on the Cross, do we wish to be crucified, that is to say, by our will and desires. The body nailed to the wood cannot do whatever it wishes or thinks. In the same way, one's thoughts nailed by divine fear remain unshaken in all its tests of patience—as one nailed to the Cross cannot think about any earthly thing, nor obey his own desires, nor is he troubled by the desire for various things, nor does he acquire care for anything earthly, nor is he exalted by pride, nor does he answer back, nor is he inflamed by hatred, nor does he grieve over material things, nor does he remember wrongs of past reproaches, but awaits departure through death for the sake of the Cross. Beware, brother, that you desire none of these things which you have renounced, having left them according to the Master's voice which said: *No man, having put his hand to the plough and looking back, is fit for the kingdom of God* (Luke 9:62). He who descends again from a lofty life to the earthly things of this world is a transgressor of Christ's commandments. When such thoughts come upon you, confess them at the very outset, in this way you will destroy the demon's foothold. Do not be ashamed to confess them to your father so that you will be able to crush the demon's head. It is not a small fall which results from lazy and obstinate thoughts.

The bearing of offenses and the deprivation of all earthly goods produces humility: first, mortify your own will; second, hide nothing from your spiritual father—not just your actions, but your thoughts as well; third, trust not your own conscience but your father's discretion and directions, even thirsting for his instruction and heeding it with delight; fourth, obey his directions in everything; fifth, not only do not dare to dishonor someone, but if dishonor should come to you from another, you must receive it with joy; sixth, do not undertake to do anything except that which is commanded by your spiritual father, even if you have heard it from the Holy Scripture; seventh, be content with even the meanest clothing; eighth, again, reckon yourself with a truthful heart to be the least of all; ninth, restrain your tongue and do not prolong conversations, neither exalt your voice pompously; tenth, do not be ready to be the first to laugh. In this spiritual rule of the goal of the common life, may you keep this all in remembrance, as David said: *As for me, like a deaf man I heard them not, and was as a speechless man that openeth not his mouth. And I became as a man that heareth not and that hath in his mouth no reproofs* (Ps. 37:13-14).

If any reproach or derision or evil revilement is brought against you, like one who is deaf be not moved nor grow angry. Meditate continually upon the words of this psalm within you: *I said I will take heed to my ways lest I sin with my tongue. I set a guard for my mouth when the sinner stood up against me* (Ps. 38:1-2). Do not hate or judge others to be more stupid or ignorant than yourself, according to the Apostle's word, *Be careful, watch* (cf. I Peter 4:7), that you be wise, showing that without deliberation or doubting you are ready to do what your father has commanded you. But with all simplicity and faith impute everything commanded by the holy man to be holy, wise, and profitable. By such obedience your heart will be strengthened.

Your patience will not be brought about by the virtues of other men; that is to say, when they are angered by someone or reproached or despised; but rather, by when you are reproached, despised or slandered, and you endure with meekness and humility.

10. STAY PUT!

He who wishes to drive demons away from himself, let him first not serve the passions.

A brother said, "I wish to depart from the place where I am living." The Abbot replied to him, "My child, this is because you have neither the Kingdom of Heaven in your mind nor the eternal torments. If you had these in your mind you would not permit yourself even to leave your cell."

11. A FALSE VIRGIN GOES FROM PLACE TO PLACE

St. Syncletica said: "Many there are in the mountains who will perish thinking earthly thoughts. It is possible, being with men, to be alone in thought, and this is better than, while being alone, to be with men in thought. If in the church you live a common life, don't change this place or the defilement will be great. Just as a hen that gets off her eggs often makes them infertile, likewise the false virgin, abandoning the faith, goes from place to place. If the enemy cannot vanquish you by slander and reproach, he suggests praise and glory; if he cannot worst you by the passions, he attempts to create changes of the soul by involuntary illnesses. He brings about grave infirmities so that, when you are enfeebled by these, he may disturb the mind and the former love for God."

12. SALVATION

Our salvation comes from our neighbor, if we love God.

CHAPTER THREE

On the Monastic Life:
Exhortations from the Writings
of St. Theodore of Edessa*

1) A monk who disobeys the commands of his spiritual father is a transgressor of the fundamental vows of his renunciation. He who has embraced obedience and slain his own will with the sword of humility has indeed fulfilled the promise that he made to Christ in the presence of many witnesses. [Chapter 43]

2) The demons, the enemies of our life, are exceedingly jealous of those pursuing the ascetic way under submission to a spiritual father. Gnashing their teeth at us and devising all kinds of snares they do and suggest everything possible so as to deprive him of the fatherly bosom. They propose plausible excuses, lead them to irritation, arouse hatred for the father and show his admonitions to be rebukes, they make his words of correction seem like sharpened arrows. Why, they ask, since you are free, have you become a slave—a slave to a merciless, unwise, ignorant, undiscerning and angry man? After this they make suggestions about giving hospitality, the visitation of the sick and the giving of alms to paupers. Next they extol above measure the rewards of extreme silence and solitude, and the monastic labors. Finally, when they have received him as a captive into their own authority, they make him carry out their evil desires. [Chapter 44]

---

*These citations from St. Theodore of Edessa were printed in the 1847 edition of the writings of Elder Theodore of Sanaxar and are central to the monastic coenobitic life as taught by the Elder. They were taken from the Paisian *Dobrotolyubie (Philokalia)* in Russian. A complete English translation may be found in St. Theodoros the Great Ascetic, "A Century of Spiritual Texts," *The Philokalia: The Complete Text,* Volume Two (London: Faber and Faber, 1984). The numbers in the present edition have been supplied by the editors.

3) You who are under obedience to a spiritual father must be alert to the cunning of the enemy who wages war against you. Do not forget your promises to God, nor be defeated by the insults of the demons; do not be afraid of reproof and rebukes; do not obey evil thoughts instilled in you, nor evade the strictures of your father; do not dishonor the humble-minded and good yoke by the brazenness of self-satisfaction and self-will, but *run with patience the race that is set before* you, *looking unto Jesus the Author and Finisher of* our *faith* (Heb. 12:1-2). [Chapter 45]

4) The beginning monk, by suffering the submission of his self in the furnace and by every sorrow, becomes aflame with the Divine commandments, drowning his evil inclinations in labors, in patience and in sorrows. He becomes accustomed to obedience and becomes radiant and fit for heavenly treasures. [Chapter 46]

5) "Silence is more valuable than speech." (Elias the Presbyter and Ekdikos.)*

6) If you have abandoned worldly cares and entered the monastic struggle, you should not have a desire to have wealth for distribution to the poor. This is another trick of the evil one to lead you to vainglory, so as to fill your mind with much care. Even if you have only bread and water, with these you can still perform hospitality. Even if you do not have these, but simply accept the stranger with a warm welcome and offer him a word of consolation, you can receive the fruits of hospitality. [Chapter 50]

7) What has been said applies to monks sitting in stillness. Those under obedience to a spiritual father should have only one thing in mind—to depart in nothing from his commands. For if they achieve this, they achieve everything. [Chapter 51]

8) Always keep your death before your eyes. Recall the vanity of the world, how deceptive it is and how worthless. Reflect on the dreadful

---

*Elias the Presbyter and Ekdikos, "A Gnomic Anthology," *The Philokalia: The Complete Text,* Volume Three (London: Faber and Faber, 1984), Part 1:4, p. 34.

reckoning that is to come. How the harsh keepers of the toll houses and the enemies of our life will bring before us the actions, words and evil thoughts which we accepted and made our own. [Chapter 57]

9) The first foes in battle who array themselves against us in every way are these: the desires of the spirit of gluttony, avarice and vainglory. Indeed, from experience we come to know that it is not possible for a man to fall into sin, or be subject to a particular passion unless he has been previously wounded by one of these three giants. [Chapter 61]

10) The wedding garment is impassivity of soul. [Chapter 64]

11) Expel from yourself the spirit of talkativeness, for from it are born every dreadful passion: lying, brazenness of speech, buffoonery, mockery, slander, accusation, obscenity and absurd chatter. [Chapter 79]

12) We have been commanded to speak well of and bless those who slander or abuse us (cf. Matt. 5:44). For when we are at peace with men, we fight against the demons. [Chapter 80]

13) Do not revile your brother for his faults. For the person who does not show love towards his brother, *does not know God, for God is love* (I John 4:8). [Chapter 81]

Elder Zosima (Verkhovsky) of Siberia.

CHAPTER FOUR

*The Testimony of Elder Zosima Verkhovsky about Elder Theodore**

"DURING THE TIME of my journey with Elder Basilisk [circa 1797], we happened once to spend a certain time in the Sanaxar Monastery where we heard many wonderful things about Fr. Theodore, in the midst of which they related this to us: He once summoned a brother of the monastery who was not at peace in soul and said to him: 'I have allowed you to live amongst us for a whole year. Now you must tell me the truth. Is your soul informed that in our monastery you hope to find salvation, is your heart disposed to frank revelation of your thoughts and devotion to me or to any of our Elders?' And when this brother, falling to the feet of the Superior, acknowledged that he did not have such feelings, then the Superior said to him, 'Although you are profitable to the monastery and very needful to us (for this brother was a skilled blacksmith), it is evident that God does not will for you to remain here. Go, seek out a monastery and an elder according to your conscience and with your whole soul serve the Lord there,' and he dismissed him in peace. I imprinted this wise and spiritual discrimination of the great Theodore in my memory and in my soul."

Fr. Zosima strongly persuaded those who had passed through the one-year or three-year trial and demonstrated a firm resolve and desire and promise to remain for their whole life in devotion and in obedience to their spiritual father and to reside uninterruptedly with the community and for this purpose had been joined to the number of the coenobium, never to disregard their vows and never to leave the community.

---

*Taken from "The Sayings of and Certain Anecdotes about the Elder Schemamonk Zosima," in *The Life and Ascetic Labors of the Elder of Blessed Memory, Schemamonk Zosima: His Sayings and Extracts from His Writings* (Moscow, 1889), Part 2, no. 26, pp. 18-19.

Schema-Abbot Jerome of Sanaxar, contemporary spiritual father
in the steps of St. Theodore.

CHAPTER FIVE

Elder Theodore of Sanaxar as a Teacher of the Spiritual Life*

FATHER THEODORE OF SANAXAR crushed the head of the cunningly vainglorious serpent: He did not fast longer than the time appointed for all the brothers but when all were at table then he too sat and ate with them. However, he ate as little of the food set before him as would satisfy the needs of his body and he concealed before others his continence so that it would not be known how he refrained from eating rich foods and would not appear before men to fast. (Paraphrase of the short life of St. John of the Ladder).

No one was shown more honor than another, either those whom he had tonsured or those who had come from another monastery already having been tonsured. With the righteous Fr. Theodore, everyone was treated the same, everyone was loved equally, knowing that the monastic habit is one and the same, wherever it is worn by anyone. In the same way, the grace of Baptism is one wherever one is vouchsafed to receive it. But according to the measure of their virtue are monastics deemed worthy of reward. He instituted a rule and penances for transgressions, some were assigned a certain number of prostrations, others certain fasts. For every transgression there was an appropriate punishment: if someone missed the divine hymnody, or broke a vessel, or threw something without cause, or did something carelessly, or grieved his brother in some way, or could not restrain his tongue from speaking excessively, or did not walk meekly or humbly, or conversed in the refectory, not listening to the reading, or complained about the food, or shamelessly and brazenly glanced with his eyes hither and thither or did some other similar thing—for all such actions penances were assigned.

---

*From "The Life of Fr. Theodore" (Moscow, 1847).

Fr. Theodore's disciple Ioannicius heard from him what is written below:

He who wishes to receive the mercy of God must keep the Lord's commandments, and the commandments of God order one to turn away from evil deeds and to do good deeds (cf. Ps. 33:14).

Turn away from evil deeds.

Do not offend one another. Do not steal another man's goods, nor take anything by deceit. Do not lie. Do not have enmity between yourselves. Do not be angry. Do not remember wrongs. Do not be a prodigal. Do not be a drunkard. Do not be a mocker, one who swears, or an idle-talker. Do not be a buffoon or a dancer. Do not perform witchcraft or other heretical deeds and do not help the sick by such means.

All of this is ungodly.

Pray to God with a contrite heart that He may remit our sins, that He will order our lives according to His mercy, and thank Him for all His mercy toward us. Go to the Church of God on all feasts of the Lord. Listen to everything that the Holy Church commands us and on other days perform without laziness whatever one's task may be and give alms to the poor from one's own labors and make offerings to the Church of God. Help one another in their needs. Whoever has been at enmity with someone, forgive him without anger; endure every chance misfortune, calamity or other necessity that befalls you without sorrow, with thanksgiving to God. Always have the fear of God in your recollection, that you be not tormented eternally. Ever entreat God that He grant us to be in the Heavenly Kingdom.

All this is pleasing to God.

This is the teaching of the righteous Fr. Theodore, the restorer of the Holy Sanaxar Monastery, who was born of the nobility, of the Ushakov family, in the city of Romanov. He was tonsured quite significantly at an oral royal decree, with the personal testing and observation of the Sovereign, by hierarchical hands in the St. Alexander Nevsky Monastery. Ten years after his entrance into the monastery and after eighteen years of wandering, he was hated by the authorities and monks on account of the many who came to him for spiritual counsel. With the posting of a military watch to monitor him, he was forced to move in 1757, with royal permission, to Sarov Monastery; and from there, after one year, to

Sanaxar, which had long lain empty and in ruins. He rebuilt and surrounded it, first with a wooden structure, then, in 1767, with a stone structure financed by royal offerings and well-disposed contributors and benefactors. When the foundation stone of the main church was being laid, a wonderful event took place: a swarm of bees flew from somewhere and came to rest right on the place of the altar and allowed themselves to be collected.* Fr. Theodore gathered about eighty brothers, enjoined all to steadfastly persevere in the common life, and strictly prohibited intoxicating beverages. He exerted a great effort to renew his monastery, which had previously fallen into desolation because of the all-encompassing state liquidation of monasteries, and he established its security for future generations by securing two Imperial Edicts on behalf of the monastery, in 1764 and 1765 [for its autonomy and upkeep].

In the city of Arzamas he gathered a similar community of about 150 women [270 at the time of the publication of this book in 1847] in the Alexeyevsky Convent in that city. He was a true father to both monasteries, a good shepherd and provider, a zealous teacher of all righteousness, a never-silent rebuker of unrighteousness, and a most wise and unflattering and strict leader. To those who came to him from the surrounding region, as well as those of noble birth and high rank who travelled from afar for spiritual benefit, he was a skilled, soul-profiting spiritual physician who used no flattery. By many he was not loved, and by others cursed and persecuted from beginning to end for righteousness' sake, but he openly endured everything bravely, in Christ Who strengthened him, for fifty-two years, and he brought many to repentance before God. In old age, in his seventy-second year, he reposed after many years of illness in 1791, on February 19, on Wednesday of Cheese-fare Week, at ten o'clock in the evening, and was buried on Saturday. Before his death, in the presence of two of his disciples, for a long time he wept bitterly and cried before God inconsolably for about a quarter of an hour, saying how much he had sinned since his youth. His body, although it lay in his warm room until his burial, did not give off the odor of death.

This last section was written on January 17, 1795, by the Elder's disciple in Sanaxar, Abbot Ioannicius, retired from his duties of governing the monastery.

---

* They were collected by the future St. Herman of Alaska, then still a novice.

САНАКСАРСКIЙ МОНАСТЫРЬ

Sanaxar Monastery in the summer. View from the southeast.

III

Counsels of Elder Theodore to the Sisters of the Alexeyevsky Community

Chapel of the Resurrection, outside the monastery gates.

CHAPTER ONE

Brief Conversations of Fr. Theodore with the Novices of the Alexeyevsky Community

(From a manuscript of the Alexeyevsky Community)*

1. SELFLESS LOVE

I want to explain to you the words of Christ: *Not everyone that saith to Me: Lord, Lord, will enter into the Kingdom of Heaven; but he that doeth the will of My Father* (Matt. 7:21). Let none of you think: we go to God's church, we pray, we make a lot of prostrations, and for this we will receive the Heavenly Kingdom. No, he will receive it who keeps God's commandments. The first is to love God with all one's heart and all one's soul and with all one's mind; and the second is to love one's neighbor as oneself—to live not just for oneself but to serve one's neighbor. Not to love anything earthly, that is, not to have any worldly attachments. If you live like this, in fulfilling God's commandments, then you will draw to yourself the Spirit of God. But if you do not live in such a way, you will attract the spirit of the adversary.

2. REMEMBRANCE OF GOD

Christ said: *Every idle word that men shall speak, they shall give account thereof in the day of judgment* (Matt. 12:36). And the Apostle of Christ said: *Grieve not the Holy Spirit of God, whereby ye are sealed unto the*

---

*These counsels were addressed to the sisters before Mother Martha's entry into this convent. They have been taken by the editors from *Counsels of Elders* (Moscow, 1913), pp. 395–413. Section titles have been provided by the editors.

day of redemption (Eph. 4:30), and again: *Let no corrupt communication proceed out of your mouth* (Eph. 4:29). That is, do not tell any kind of jokes, do not make fun of anything—this is fitting only for worldly people, and you call yourselves monastics. Why have you come to the monastery? Think about it! I know that several of you do not want to keep quiet about another sister, and that you envy one another. This distracts you from the remembrance of God. The spirit of the adversary will make you his own inasmuch as the passions are in you: envy, hatred, remembrance of evil, reproach, mockery, deceit, idleness, sloth, blasphemy; all this is in you and binds the spirit of impurity to your soul. How many times have I told you and travelled here for this purpose? I labor so that you would have holy love, patience and silence amongst yourselves ... and would quit idle talkativeness. Others think only about rest and about how someone offended them in some way, but the remembrance of God is not to be found in them. I have always told you that your prayers and prostrations will be useless if you do not live according to the commandments of the Lord.... Remember what I have said and acquire for yourselves the Spirit of God, and ask God that He would give you repentance before the end.

3. RAISING THE MIND TO GOD

I have heard that many of you say, "We receive alms but we do not pray, that is, we seldom go to church, due to which we have lost hope that we will receive God's mercy." It seems that I have always told you that prayer doesn't consist solely in your prostrations, but that your good deeds facilitate prayer. One can pray always and everywhere, walking or sitting.... Prayer is the raising of the mind to God, during which one must ask His goodness for the remission of sins, saying: "O Lord! take away my sins from me and deprive me not of Thy loving-kindness; grant me victory and mastery over the enemy and over all the passions." One must ask God's aid in this way and personally live uprightly. I have always been telling you: your prayer will be useless if you will not live well; if you pray but do not make an effort to ammend your life and instead live in slothfulness, then your prayer will be nothing.

4. THE ONE THING NEEDFUL

We have read that one must seek the precious stone. What is this? It is Christ the Savior. With what and how must one seek? Through a good monastic life. This saying concerns you, for you live in a monastery, and for this reason you have come to the monastery, to seek Christ. It is written: "Sell all that you have, but buy the one priceless pearl (stone)" (cf. Matt. 13:46), that is, forsake all the passions, and above all your own will, and seek out this stone. The Lord has said: *So let your light so shine before men, that they may see your good works, and glorify your Father which is in Heaven* (Matt. 5:16). This saying refers (primarily) to you, so that your (monastic) life might be light, not darkness. All laymen point to those in monasteries, at how they live, and emulate what is good in them. *If the light that is in thee be darkness,* said the Saviour, *how great is that darkness!* (Matt. 6:23). When those living in monasteries falter, changing the light of their lives into darkness, then how much more does this affect laymen? Monastics are called a light because by their good lives they must give an example to laymen. In order to be a light, they must have love one for another, submission, humility. The Apostle says: *My little children, of whom I travail in birth again until Christ be formed in you* (Gal. 4:19), that is, I sorrow until such a time that your lives will be in harmony with the commandments of Christ. This saying concerns me so much, that I would that this sorrow over your lives not reach me. For this reason, have I travelled to see you. I worry, I converse with you in my calling as your instructor in order to teach you the saving path. Let each one of you examine her own conscience and remember and carry out what I have taught you.

5. KNOWLEDGE OF THE TRUTH

The holy Apostle said: [They] *are ever learning, and never able to come to the knowledge of the truth* (II Tim. 3:7). These words mean: here you, for example, are always hearing the word of God but in your deeds you do not fulfill what you have heard. You lead a life not according to the guidance of the

Word of God, and because of this you are not able to come to a knowledge of the truth, and you live in negligence of your monastic calling. Above all, love should abide among you one for another, and submission, humility, and patience. The Lord demands these virtues from us but does not ask much. Because of your lack of discretion, you discuss prolonged fasts and your inability to go to God's temple on weekdays, but God does not require this of you who are bound by the labors of the common life.

6. SOBRIETY BEFORE HOLY COMMUNION

The holy Apostle says concerning those who receive Holy Communion: *Wherefore whosoever shall eat this bread, and drink this cup of the Lord, unworthily ... eateth and drinketh damnation to himself* (I Cor. 11:27, 29). *For this cause many are weak and sickly among you, and many sleep* (I Cor. 11:30). They sleep not a bodily sleep, but one of the soul. They do not take care for the salvation of the soul. A careless life and passionate attachment to the world is called the sleep of night. Those who live that way revel in the passionate delights of the world, and therefore the Apostle calls them sickly in soul because of their sins, and they truly partake unworthily. If a man approaches the Holy Mysteries with discrimination, in repentance and contrition of heart over his sins, has the intention not to sin and prays, "O Lord, I am sinful and unworthy to approach Thy great and awesome Mystery, but trusting in Thy great compassion, I intend with Thy help to correct my life according to Thy holy commandments and to turn away from sin," such a man can truly partake worthily.

7. CONSCIENTIOUS CHURCH ATTENDANCE

One must go to the church of God with the aim of hearing what is being read and sung, and what the Church of God enjoins us to do, we must resolve to fulfill in actual fact. The church is the Christian school, and it is not our words that are pleasing to God, even though they be words of prayer, but together with our prayers good deeds as well.

8. LOVE OF THIS WORLD IS DEATH

The man who loves the world is like a corpse. A corpse has no needs—if it is beaten, it feels nothing. In like manner does the devil lead the passionate lovers of the world to perdition, killing the soul through sin, beating it. But he feels nothing, and goes wherever his useless passions lead him.

9. WORLDLINESS IS POISON

If tasty morsels were being offered to someone, and at the bottom of them deadly poison had been concealed, then I suppose that no one knowing about this would choose to taste them, since poison had been hidden underneath—even if the food were sweet. Such are the unseemly delights of the world—parties, promenades, music and all the other empty demonic entertainments. There is spiritual poison in them and the poor man doesn't see it and cannot break away from their ungodliness.

10. THE HOLINESS OF NATIVITY

The feast of the Nativity of Christ is being celebrated but, I think that rare is he who understands the full spiritual significance of this celebration. Every feast of God must be viewed from its spiritual side. What majesty there is in the Birth of Christ—unapproachable and unfathomable to our understanding. The Lord took upon Himself our human nature and nothing other than love for fallen mankind inclined His loving-kindness to take upon Himself corruptible flesh. Being clothed in flesh, He bore upon Himself all the infirmities of mankind (except sin), so that mankind would not be able to excuse himself because of the difficulty of fulfilling the Lord's commandments and would not say, "Thou, O Lord, hast placed upon us that which we cannot bear." Thus Christ took upon Himself our flesh and made Himself an example of how we must live, so that we may not excuse ourselves by claiming that it is impossibile to do. The Lord opened the doors of Paradise to us, which had been closed by the sin of our forefather

(Adam). Behold with what spiritual understanding we must celebrate and thank God's goodness for all His compassions toward us. But (sinful) people, in place of a spiritual celebration, invent an idolatrous celebration for themselves, turning their love toward the world and its passions: riches, luxury and gluttony. The poor lovers of the world cannot see their own perdition in this.

11. THANKFULNESS TO GOD

I remembered God and I was gladdened (Ps. 76:3). This is the meaning of these words: with his noetic eyes the Psalmist began to observe God's creation, how it was all created by His wisdom, unfathomable to the human mind: the heavens are stretched out, the earth is made steadfast, the winds blow, the waters flow, the seas stand within their bounds. Gazing at all this wonderful creation, the Psalmist cries out: *Thy knowledge is too wonderful for me; it is mighty, I cannot attain unto it* (Ps. 138:5). That is, Thy knowledge is wonderful, exalted far beyond me, I cannot attain unto Him, Thy wisdom is inaccessible to my limited understanding. Knowing from the creation the Creator who has created all things in wisdom, the Psalmist turns his gaze to man, seeing God's love towards him and His great compassions and benefactions, but his own baseness. Therefore he said: *I am a worm* (before God), *and not a man* (Ps. 21:6). God's love toward corruptible man compelled the Psalmist to be ever thankful to God for all His mercies which He showed in his life, spending it in the fulfilling of God's commandments, loving nothing earthly more than God, and always burning for Him in spirit, in the hope that God would abide with him inseparably. Therefore, he said: *I remembered God and I was gladdened,* and he did not merely remember, but lived a life in harmony with the will of God, in the hope of His loving-kindness and the reception of future blessings. During times of misfortune the Prophet David remembered God and was thereby comforted. Enduring persecution from Saul and then from his own son Absalom, with hope in God's loving-kindness, he found all consolation in God and said: *I beheld the Lord ever before me, for He is at my right hand* (Ps. 15:8), *therefore did my heart rejoice* (Ps. 15:9). He knew that the Lord was always with him and therefore he said: *Though I should walk in the midst of the valley of the shadow of death, I will fear no evil, for Thou art with me* (Ps. 22:4).

Thus, the prophetic word is fitting for you (sisters), for us, and for every man. One must bear with patience and thanksgiving everything that befalls us in hope of God's loving-kindness. He who lives uprightly (according to God's commandments) must hope in God's goodness, remembering the prophetic words: *I remembered God and I was gladdened,* and to those who live in carelessness these words do not apply, for they have no joy in God. I know this about you sisters: you sit without leaving the monastery, you labor day and night (in handiwork, obediences and at prayer), and therefore I say this prophetic word to you in consolation: *I remembered God and I was gladdened.* As one lives, so too will he receive recompense, depending on his life.

12. REMEMBRANCE OF DEATH

There is a picture depicting a man sitting and contemplating: "Time is passing by, flying as if on wings, and three sorrows have seized me. The first, that death lies before me. The second, that I don't know exactly when the hour of my death will come. The third, that after death I don't know where I will find myself—amidst the number of those shown mercy or amidst the condemned." Every man must keep this picture before his physical and noetic eyes.

13. GIVE GLORY TO GOD

Let not thy left hand know what thy right hand doeth (Matt. 6:3). If you do some good deed, do not join any kind of craftiness of the adversary to it. While offering a prayer or alms, let them not be offered with vainglory or man-pleasing. In fasting and prayers, do not fall into high-mindedness. While doing any good deed, do not call attention to yourself: do not think that you are doing anything great; do not ascribe it to yourself, but to God's help. If you do something good, it is not by your own power but through God who has helped you. You cannot of yourself think anything good without God. Ascribe what is good to God and only what is evil to yourself.

14. SUBJECT THE FLESH TO THE SPIRIT!

The Lord Jesus Christ said to His Apostles: *Watch and pray that ye enter not into temptation* (Matt. 26:41). With these words the Lord urges us all to prayer that through it we may escape the temptations of the enemy; for, without prayer and calling upon God's help, it is impossible to be delivered from the assaults of the enemy. He afterwards added further: *The Spirit indeed is willing, but the flesh is weak ... sleep on now, and take your rest* (Matt. 26:41, 45). This was said because the Apostles, although in spirit, out of love for Christ wished to keep watch with Him, to be inseparably beside Him, yet their infirm flesh made war against them. Therefore the Lord commands everyone to pray and to call on God's help so as to subject the flesh to the spirit with the help of God's grace.

15. BLASPHEMOUS THOUGHTS

Many cannot distinguish between what are blasphemous thoughts and what are vile thoughts. Vile and abominable thoughts are called blasphemous by many people and because of this many are led to despair. Blasphemous thoughts originate from pride. For example, someone begins to think about Christ, that Christ had such a human (infirm) nature and flesh. He begins to debase Him (as did Arius), and finally conceives an extremely high opinion of himself, deriding everything and everyone. Or, he begins to say that God's saints were also weak people and in his pride he does not wish to acknowledge them (this is precisely what the Protestants do). Blasphemous thoughts are born from such mad pride. But vile and abominable thoughts are those which issue, either from an impure life, or from wicked habits, or from the suggestion of the enemy. For example, if someone speaks of God, the saints or the holy icons with vile words, such thoughts can overcome everyone but they cannot harm a man. In the same way that the wind blows and passes by, so these vile thoughts pass by like the wind if a man does not consent to them.

16. THE POWER OF THE WORD OF GOD

Two-edged swords shall be in their hands (Ps. 149:6). *The Word of God is … sharper than any two-edged sword* (Heb. 4:12). The Word of God passes within a man. Many slay themselves with the Scripture as with a sword; namely, they do not catch its meaning as it should be understood but, rather, interpret it according to their own fancy (and not according to the understanding of the Holy Church and the Fathers). From this, heresy can arise. Or, someone will attempt to fulfill the commandments of the Scripture in a way that is above his strength and beyond measure, and falls into despair being unable to fulfill them in that way. One should keep oneself from such extremes so that, instead of being saved, he does not perish by the sword of the Word of God.

17. THE JUDGMENT OF GOD

I will judge uprightly (Ps. 74:2). This signifies that if a man does something good and thinks: I have accomplished a great task, I am righteous before God, then the Lord will judge such righteousness, that is, our good deeds accomplished with vainglory or high-mindedness or self-praise before men. If we ascribe good deeds to ourselves and not to God, for this we will be judged.

Chapter Two

The Rule of the Alexeyevsky Community

The charter rule given by Fr. Theodore and observed in detail in the community until the present time [1866], consists in the following rules:

1) All novices who live in the coenobium must be in absolute obedience without contradiction to the Superior.

2) Each sister must live in the cell assigned by the Superior, persevering in the labors and handiwork deemed appropriate for her.

3) Food, clothing and every provision is to be held in common; to have something in one's personal possession or separately from the community is strictly forbidden.

4) Every luxury, worldly entertainment, or excessive decoration of the cell is strictly forbidden, just as is the use of anything silk or colored, other than cotton or wool material of exclusively black color.

5) None of the sisters has the right to make anything for her own profit, or to work separately for herself. In general, all labors, work and handicrafts are to be performed by all for the common good.

6) Everyone without exception is obliged to be at the morning and evening prayer rule conducted daily, except the infirm and those for whom it is not possible to leave their obediences. At the morning prayer rule, which is always to begin at about four in the morning, morning prayers, the two appointed kathismata and the general commemoration are to be read. At the evening prayer rule, at eight or nine in the evening on weekdays, but earlier on Sundays and feast days, Compline is to be read with the Canon to Sweetest Jesus and the Akathist to the Mother of God. A set number of prostrations are to be made. An instructive homily from the writings of the Holy Fathers, the general commemoration, evening prayers and an Akathist appointed for that day are to be read. On feast days, in addition to the aforementioned, all the stichera and irmoi of the feast are to be chanted.

On Sundays and feast days all the sisters without exception are to go to the church services; while on weekdays only the aged and infirm, as well as those at essential obediences are to be excused.

7) Almost from the very beginning of the community, the unceasing, uninterrupted (by turns) reading of the Psalter in a separate, tidy cell was instituted for the health of the Emperor and his family, for the Holy Synod, the Diocesan bishop and as well for the benefactors of the community. In another cell there is the reading of the Psalter for the repose of the Emperors and Empresses, for hierarchs and individual Orthodox Christians whose names have been inscribed in the commemoration book. These readings of the Psalter do not cease either by day or by night and they are not omitted even on feast days.

8) Everyone is obliged to come in common to the refectory for lunch and dinner at the ringing of the bell, excepting the aged and infirm, for whom a separate meal is arranged in the infirmary church. Concerning the quality and quantity of food in the refectory, the monastic church rule is observed precisely on Mondays, Wednesdays and Fridays throughout the whole year. Likewise during the fasts, excluding allowances set forth in the typicon, a meal is served once a day. During the course of the meal there is a reading of Patristic books as assigned by the Superior.

9) Without the blessing and special direction of the Superior, no one is allowed, for even the shortest time, to leave the convent enclosure. For obediences to be performed outside the monastery, that is, for the purchase at markets of everything necessary for the feeding and sustenance of the sisters, and for other needs of the community as well, the Superior is to utilize the older sisters who are known to be more experienced in their manner of life.

10) Besides the Superior's quarters, as well as the guesthouse for visitors and the rooms adjoining the gates for simple folk, no one of the male sex, under any pretext, is allowed to enter the other cells, though he be even the closest relative. Visitors can see and speak with those novices living in the monastery only in the above-mentioned guesthouse and rooms by the entrance, and in the presence of the older sisters of sound morals who live in these cells.

None of those living in the community, from the Superior to the novices, according to the testament of Elder Theodore, needs to have to have been tonsured.

CHAPTER THREE

Counsels to the Sisters of the Alexeyevsky Community

1. DESIRE

I remembered God and I was gladdened (Ps. 76:3), and what greater joy can there be than to remember God? The Scriptures say: *Except the Lord build the house* of the virtues, *in vain do they labor that build it* (Ps. 126:1); and again: *No one can come to Me, except* My *Father ... draw him* (John 6:44). This means that without God's holy help one cannot accomplish anything good; and since His help is always ready, He requires from us the desire and care for what is good.

2. THE GIFT OF GOD

Every man hath his proper gift of God (I Cor. 7:7), that is, one much, another little, not because God has so willed, but because to the extent that a man labors, he receives a corresponding gift. If one has expended great care and labor, to the same measure of his toil will he receive recompense (cf. II Cor. 9:6).

3. LOSING GRACE

It is said in the Gospel that *every idle word that men shall speak, they shall give account thereof in the day of judgment* (Matt. 12:36). And again: *Let no corrupt communication,* that is, idle communication, *proceed out of your mouth ... and grieve not the Holy Spirit of God, whereby ye are sealed* (Eph. 4:29, 30). For the Holy Spirit is grieved and departs from a man who speaks idle and blasphemous words, and when the Holy Spirit is grieved and departs, then the spirit of deceit comes to a man; and seeing him empty, deprived of the grace of God, he enters him and leads him, according to his desire, into destructive passions.

4. LABOR TO INCREASE GRACE!

Whosoever hath, to him shall be given and given in abundance; *and whosoever hath not, from him shall be taken even that which he seemeth to have* (Luke 8:18). This signifies the grace of God given at baptism. If a man loses this by his depraved manner of life, then there shall be taken from him what he presumes to have; that is, the grace given at baptism. And, to a man who through his life takes care and labors to increase the grace given to him, it shall be given and given in abundance, according to his God-pleasing life.

5. CHRIST

Verily I say unto you: Among them that are born of women there hath not risen a greater than John the Baptist; notwithstanding, he that is least in the Kingdom of Heaven is greater than he! (Matt. 11:11). Who is this, who being least in the Kingdom of Heaven, is greater than he (John)? Of course, it is Christ Himself. Inasmuch as the people considered him less than the Baptist, He afterwards said about Himself: he that is least in the Kingdom of Heaven is greater than he.

6. RESOLVE VERSUS FAINTHEARTEDNESS

Whoever enters the monastery with the determination to endure all things for the sake of God, the same builds his house upon a rock (cf. Matt. 7:24, 25), and if a trial befalls him, if the wind blows against the house, it will not be shaken, for it is founded upon a rock, that is, upon resolute determination. Whoever goes to the monastery without such an understanding, but thinks about how long he might live there, that he has not come for good and can leave, has built his house upon the sand (cf. Matt. 7:26, 27). If even the slightest temptation befalls him, like the wind, then he is not only shaken, but is hurled out of the monastery, since the house of his life was founded upon the sand, that is, not upon steadfast determination.

7. WE CAN STAND UP AGAINST PASSIONS

We are not able to thank and praise God as is meet, but to entreat His favor to grant us His aid against our enemies and against the passions is possible for all.

8. JUDGING

There are three types of judging: 1) When you learn of some secret sin and tell everyone; 2) When you begin to debase a person because of a sin to such an extent that you don't wish to speak with him; 3) When you condemn a sinner to absolute perdition, as did that elder [Isaac of Thebes, as recounted in the *Alphabetical Patericon*] condemned, and to whom an angel of God brought the soul of the condemned sinner and asked: where do you command this soul to be placed—in paradise, or in torment? From this the elder came to his senses.* But, when seeing a bad action, you begin thinking that someone is doing wrong, this will not be considered judging, but discrimination, and thereby, of course you will not sin.

---

*Cited from Abba Dorotheus, "On Refusal to Judge our Neighbor," in *Discourses and Sayings* (Kalamazoo, Michigan: Cistercian Publications, 1977), p. 133.

Chapter Four

Letters to the Sisters from Solovki

WHEN Fr. Theodore was sentenced to exile at the Solovki Monastery, deprived of the priestly rank, the sorrow and tears of his disciples in the Alexeyevsky Community were so bitter and intense that they prompted the loving Elder to write some consolation to his spiritual daughters. We present here three letters of the Elder written to the sisters in the community.*

LETTER ONE

The mercy of God be with you!

My separation from you now has come to pass, but you, of course, should not sorrow about this, since everything is accomplished not without the will of God, and we cannot oppose it, nor can we fathom God's Providence for us. Most of all we must know that the Divine judgments lead us to perfect patience, without which there is no salvation for us. So do not grieve but rejoice that God's goodness has led us to such sorrow, the more so, that it has come absolutely blamelessly, and that it is only for the reproach of human unrighteousness and for injustice which cries out to heaven, that we, out of our obligation, must always speak of this and not only suffer but be prepared even to die. Although we suffer, yet we offer thanks for everything to the goodness of the Lord Most High and entrust you all to the Creator for safekeeping.

The brotherhood has been instructed concerning your upkeep.

Hieromonk Theodore
June 12, 1774

---

* In another source these letters are addressed to Maria Petrovna Protasieva: "Letters of Fr. Theodore Ushakov to Maria Petrovna Protasieva, the Superior of the Arzamas Alexeyevsky Community," in *Russian Monk,* no. 11, June 1913, pp. 661–674. Inasmuch as she was not living in the community until after his return from Solovki, this cannot be considered accurate.

LETTER TWO

The mercy of God be with you all!

Now I inform you that my final banishment from you to the Solovki Monastery has taken place. I ask you not to sorrow over this but to place your hope absolutely on the Lord's will, since whatever happens takes place, of course, not without God's will. Not only am I not hereby embittered, but even rejoice that from many sorrows I have received freedom and absolute rest for my spirit. I entrust you all to God's safekeeping.

God's blessing be with you all.

Monk Theodore
July 19, 1774

They have taken away the priesthood, but God's mercy they cannot take away.

LETTER THREE

The mercy of God be with you!

I received your letter in which I hear only your cry of sorrow over my banishment [exile to Solovki].

You will only anger the Lord God more through this. I have always commented to you about this, that you would submit to His holy will in everything. How can you oppose what He has ordained? We sin much through despondency and improper sorrow. You write that you are trying to gather testimony about your noble rank in order to acquire free residency. Although it will be possible, it is nevertheless still not needed at present. Live as long as you can in one place. They haven't sent me into exile (to Siberia) yet, nor do you, my friend, need to wander far after me. An eternal road is prepared for all of us. May God grant that we might walk this road unharmed, that we may be there together eternally. Concerning this ask the Lord's grace, and thus do not wander much; perhaps in time everything will pass.

God's blessing be with you!

CHAPTER FIVE

Counsels to Schema-Abbess Martha and the Sisters of the Alexeyevsky Community

(A fragment of a manuscript preserved in the convent.)

FATHER THEODORE told me [Schema-Abbess Martha]* that "the Lord God does not require your tears and contrition but demands your deeds, so likewise do I say unto you: Try to show your love in deeds, that is, by obedience and patience, and not by tears.... You, my friend, poorly understand the crumbs of the Fathers. Because of this, every little thing leads you into great sorrow.

"Christ does not lie by my fatherly lips—you will be eternally consoled, if for a time you nobly bear fatherly obedience.

"The prayers of one's father are a shelter over our heads which protect us!"

With all my soul I wish to serve the holy monastery in obedience to Christ, to my father [Theodore] and my sisters and through my father's prayers I hope to receive some forgiveness of my sins. For my beloved father gave me hopes that the cares (the responsibilities borne by a Mother Superior) in which I find myself will present me before God.

Listen to the Elder's instructions. He did not say keep weeping, but directed us to have obedience above all else, and thence love will come. Believe this without doubting!

If you will heed our most wise instructor (Fr. Theodore), believe that he will lead us to the Lord, only bear with love the crosses placed on us by his fatherly compassion, and do not tire!

---

*Schema-Abbess Martha (in the world Maria Petrovna Protasieva), Superior of the Alexeyevsky Community from 1785 to 1813.

The Elder's counsels and mine cannot be a consolation to you when you forsake holy obedience. May God preserve you!

1) "I myself know [says Fr. Theodore] how difficult human shame is from the reproach of another, but if you nobly accept my obedience, you will receive great mercy from the Lord God and eternal not temporal recompense. For I know how much you have endured, for which I love such ones dearly and wish that they might receive God's eternal mercy."

2) "You ask for an explanation of my words which I wrote to you about Communion of the Holy Mysteries; about such people who are disposed to spend their entire life carelessly, even to the threshold of death, and receive the Holy Mysteries, yet they do not reveal their sins and do not repent of them at all. In regard to such do the Apostle's words refer: *Whosoever shall eat this bread* (the Body of Christ), *or drink this cup of the Lord* (His Blood), *unworthily, shall be guilty of the Body and Blood of the Lord. ... He that eateth and drinketh unworthily, eateth and drinketh damnation to himself,...* from this *many are weak and sickly among you, and many sleep* (I Cor. 11:27-30), that is, have become darkened, not enlightened. If such ones in their carelessness and at the end of their life commune of the Holy Mysteries, they are still not freed from their sins, since even to their death they have spent their lives in iniquities. Communion of the Holy Mysteries can be for them a seal of Christianity and therefore through commemoration in church can receive from God a certain forgiveness and freedom. My word to you was about such ones and did not equally concern those who take great care over their life. If these people sin in some way, then by repentance and communion of the Holy Mysteries they are delivered from it, and try to preserve themselves in advance from such a fall. Thereby, communion of the Holy Mysteries gives them greater understanding and strengthens them."

3) "I have heard your conclusion that what you had gathered in [prayer in] your cell, now that you are the Superior, you have lost. In this, my friend, you have of course been deceived. You did not gather anything in your cell but simply sat in one place and now you are standing at war, so now conquer

the enemy, for it is not by sitting next to the stove that you can boast about hesychasm. This warfare and presumed disturbance is much better than your stillness. Observe for yourself, what good has your cell brought you? Truly nothing! Now when you go forth to do battle, it behooves you not to grow bored, but to learn every aspect of warfare, that is, obedience, humility and patience. Only sin must be accounted as a misfortune of the soul, while my separation from you cannot and must not be misfortune for you, inasmuch as your teacher, first of all, is the Lord and then the Divine law. Fear to sin out of ignorance, but the Lord will not be angry at whomever sins in ignorance. Above all, beware of negligence and sloth."

4) "You write about your illness and that you expect death. So if by God's will death comes, I release you. Go in peace and have hope of receiving the Lord's mercy on account of your obedience to us and your clear conscience. But if you have at some time murmured and grown slothful, I forgive you this, and the Lord will not require it of you! You think that inasmuch as your illness is linked to sorrow, it will not be beneficial to you. Your opinion is not sound. From whatever cause an illness comes about, if you bear it patiently, and at the same time believe that it has been sent to you from God, then it will be absolutely beneficial. I wish to let you depart with joy to the most compassionate Father and Lord. I know your soul, and for this reason I let you go with hope to receive God's mercy. Tell the sisters not to grieve over your death, but rather to accept the will of the Lord, and to take pains over their own souls and to desire to see you not only for a time but eternally and to entreat the Lord's goodness for this."

5) "You have written to me about your sins, frankly stating that you have sinned much, and you ask from me some penance for this. I will speak thus: Punish yourself with the fear of God and believe that for everything you have done, the wrath of God will come upon you, that if you do not now make the determination henceforth to correct yourself, your life will be cut short. Then what answer will you give before God? I now forgive all this, but if you will not preserve yourself from this in the future, you will greatly provoke the Lord God to wrath. You write that two sisters left and a third was barely able to restrain herself. You blame yourself that they left because of

your strictness. Such reasoning of yours proceeds from your extreme lack of understanding. Many depraved people have separated themselves from Christ. Is Christ to blame? Many have turned away from God's saints. Are the saints to blame? How empty, my friend, is your reasoning! I tell you that not only if two or three have left, even if there are several of them, let us not grieve in vain over the careless. But I charge you to see to it that there be no willfulness. What kind of joy is there for me to support a multitude of the disobedient who have no desire to serve God? They must be taught absolute obedience and the cutting off of their own will."

6) Conversing, as was his custom, with his spiritual daughters and sisters in the community, Fr. Theodore commented on the Psalm [136]: *By the waters of Babylon,* with particular contrition and tears, saying: "When the sons of Israel, deprived of their fatherland Jerusalem, and not seeing the least consolation anywhere in a foreign land, sat as strangers by the waters of Babylon and wept, by this weeping they offered a figure of the state of all amidst misfortune and sorrow who dwell upon the earth. We, too, must keep in our thoughts that we in this impoverished life are like sojourners, ever pursued and worn out by misfortunes from our enemies; only then will we find consolation for ourselves when we remember the Sion on high: *I remembered God and I was gladdened* (Ps. 76:3)." During this contrite and parting conversation as it were, everyone wept—both the Superior and her sisters.

7) "Someone wants to complain to the bishop that the Superior doesn't allow her to pray to God. Let her present the matter as she wishes. Then we can give the following answer: if we do not labor, but are always praying to God (that is, going to church), then we will not have anything with which to feed ourselves; since we are not given any funds, there will be nothing to do except starve. But, we do not prohibit anyone from praying, aside from the fact that we order them to labor. We are exhorted by God to pray [in common in church] on Sundays and feast days, but on the other simple days we are without fail obliged by God to labor to feed ourselves and other unfortunate ones who request our help."

Sunset at Sanaxar Monastery, during the time of the spring flooding, giving the monastery the appearance of an island on a lake.

8) "See to it that your spiritual flock is not harmed. I have heard of several cases of your laxity which may have appeared good, but were in actuality worthless. You simply have not perceived them for what they are. I heard that during processions with the Icon [probably the Orans Mother of God], young people hastily came to the Icon in a highly disordered manner, in extremely crowded conditions, during which time there were plenty of people of the male sex (visitors and pilgrims). Likewise, during encounters and departures there has been much that has not been good, and I heard that other young women went with the Icon to other churches. This is even worse, for they were absolutely idle onlookers, and you don't understand this. I forgive you this now, but exercise caution in the future. I am always ordering you to look after the novices, so that they might not be idle spectators, but would sit more often in their places so as to remember the Lord God. The Theotokos does not want to see them wander, but chiefly wants them to sit in their place. Thus you should strive hard to do this and not let them have their will."

Sanaxar Monastery from the southwest.

Senior monks of the Sanaxar Monastery leaving the church in procession.

IV

Letters to Schema-Abbess Martha

Schema-Abbess Martha in her coffin (†1813).

CHAPTER ONE

Righteous Schema-Abbess Martha

(MARIA PETROVNA PROTASIEVA)
Commemorated April 30 (†1813)

THE FLOURISHING STATE of the monastic life in Russian convents in the nineteenth century owes its due to Schema-Abbess Martha, whose close contact with the great Elder Theodore of Sanaxar and St. Paisius Velichkovsky made the perennial Orthodox ascetic tradition accessible to enterprising young women of all social classes.

Born on March 2, 1760, Maria Petrovna Protasieva, the daughter of an eminent noble family in the Kostroma Province, secretly left home at a tender age hoping to enter upon the monastic path in a neighboring convent, but was discovered by her father's servants before reaching her desired goal. Soon, however, she won her family's approval and was able to enter a nearby convent in Kostroma.

She once chanced to meet two monks from Sanaxar, who were on their way to Solovki to see their spiritual father, Theodore, about whom they told her much. Desiring a true spiritual instructor, she made a pilgrimage to Solovki to seek the guidance of Elder Theodore, who was kept there in banishment. She visited him several times in Solovki. When Elder Theodore was later able to return to Sanaxar, she transferred to the Alexeyevsky Coenobitic Women's Community in Arzamas (seventy miles from Sanaxar), living there in complete obedience to the Elder, revealing to him her thoughts and the secrets of her heart. In 1786 Elder Theodore entrusted to her the guidance of the sisters in the community, which at one time numbered as many as seven hundred sisters.

Having lived peacefully for two years, she then began to experience great affliction of soul. Soon, in 1791, to add to her sorrow, Elder Theodore

An old print of Elder Theodore
recently found in Russia.

died. An orphan, she wrote to St. Paisius Velichkovsky, revealing her grief and the affliction of her heart. Elder Paisius, in reply, sent her his classic epistle (see Letter One) on holy obedience according to the teaching of the Fathers, and exhorted her to persevere in guiding the sisters in all humility, in serving as an example of the common life and in the reading of Patristic books. She even attempted to go to join his sisters, but his repose prevented it. After the death of St. Paisius a correspondence continued between her and his successor, Sophronius, as well as with Schemamonk Athanasius, who had been an assistant in the publication of *The Philokalia* in 1794.

Schema-Abbess Martha reposed on April 30, 1813. Her relics were uncovered several years later and were found to be incorrupt. Her portraits are painted as icons with traditional scrolls, citing her teaching as a monastic leader, just as she had served for generations.

CHAPTER TWO

A Letter of St. Paisius

M. P. Protasieva (Martha in schema), after the death of her spiritual father, Elder Theodore, in 1791, appealed for spiritual instruction to Elder Paisius Velichkovsky, whom she knew to be teaching the same Patristic doctrine of monasticism as her own Elder. Elder Paisius' reply to her is one of the classic expressions of true monastic life, founded on holy obedience. The main points of her biography, relating to her monastic path, are given in this letter.*

To the Honorable Lady Maria, with her God-gathered Sisters,
REJOICE IN THE LORD!

Christ our true God says: *I am come to send fire on the earth, and what will I if it be already kindled?* (Luke 12:49.) This Divine fire, cast on the earth of their hearts, the holy Apostles and disciples of the Lord received from Him, and being kindled with a flame of love for Him, they left the world and all that is in the world and, coming to Him as to their Lord and Teacher and true Instructor on the path of salvation, gave themselves over soul and body into true obedience and cutting off of their own will and understanding to their last breath, and with great and unutterable joy said to Him: *Behold, we have forsaken all and followed Thee* (Matt. 19:27). Having ever this Divine fire in their hearts, and in everything following the Divine will of their Lord and Teacher, they preserved this obedience as the apple of their eye (cf. Prov. 7:2) to the end of their life, sealing it with the bearing of numberless temptations and various deaths and the spilling of their blood to the last drop, which they shed for their faith and love toward Christ God so that they might preserve their obedience to Him, as a pure and immaculate sacrifice, unto death.

---

*Translated from the complete Slavonic text in the Optina edition of St. Paisius' Life (Moscow, 1847), pp. 239–247. English translation originally published in *Blessed Paisius Velichkovsky* (Platina, Calif.: St. Herman Brotherhood, 1976), pp. 202–214.

The holy Martyrs received this Divine fire of God's love and endured with unutterable joy various torments and the cruelest deaths for Christ God, receiving from Him the crown of His Divine glory in the Kingdom of Heaven. All our holy and God-bearing Fathers received this Divine fire and fled the world and all that is in the world; some of them remained in the common life in perfect obedience and cutting off of their own will to their last breath, and received a martyr's crown from the Lord's right hand; and some of them struggled in deserts and in mountains and in dens and caves of the earth (Heb. 11:38), going on the strait and narrow way, ever bearing in their body the death of the Lord Jesus (II Cor. 4:10). Being co-crucified with Christ, remaining in hunger and thirst and in every suffering of evil, in unceasing prayer and entreaties and tears, and passing their lives in the utter poverty of Christ and the Holy Apostles, and keeping the commandments of the Gospel purely and immaculately as the apple of their eye—they were vouchsafed the Kingdom of Heaven.

And what more shall I say? All the Saints received this Divine fire of God's grace, keeping with all diligence the soul-saving commandments of the Gospel, without doing which, by the Orthodox Faith alone, it is not possible to be saved. The true slaves of Christ, of every rank and calling and in every place of His dominion, thus received salvation.

This fire of the Divine love of Christ, being cast into the earth of your heart through His grace by diligent and attentive reading of certain soul-profiting books, you yourself did receive from His goodness; and thereupon you did hate the world and all that is in the world and conceive the intention to leave the world and labor unto God silently day and night in the unmarried life. Your father, after discovering your intention, strove by every means to divert you from it, and brought every kind of persecution against you, wishing to quench the fire of Divine zeal in your soul; but, with the cooperation of God's grace, you overcame everything by your patience, so that your father himself, despairing of keeping you longer in the world and seeing your firm intention to leave the world and labor unto God, let you go to the monastery in Kostroma. Remaining there for four years, being inspired to this by God's grace, you were enabled to read a multitude of Patristic books, from reading which you received such profit for the soul that you desired the common life and entreated Christ the Saviour to grant you a true instructor, with the promise that if you found a perfect instructor you would, in accordance with the teaching of St. Basil the Great, St. John of the Ladder and St. Simeon the New Theologian, give yourself over to him in complete obedience of soul and body, hating and renouncing all your desire and will, so as to be trampled upon by everyone in the common life.

Christ, the Seer of hearts, fulfilling this intention of yours and your entreaty concerning it, since in all respects it was good and God-pleasing, gave you a true instructor unto salvation, the reposed Fr. Theodore of blessed memory. Hearing about him, you travelled to him on the island of Solovki. The Lord returned him to his coenobitic monastery, and then he had another monastery, a coenobitic one for women, some seventy miles from his men's monastery; and to this coenobitic women's monastery in Arzamas you transferred from your previous State-recognized monastery in Kostroma. There you remained with the holy sisters in complete obedience to this holy man and in the cutting off of your own will and understanding in everything, in accordance with the Divine Scriptures and the tradition and teaching of our Holy Fathers, receiving the teaching from him as from the mouth of God and submitting to him in everything, not as to a man but as to Christ God Himself, confessing to him, when he travelled from his own monastery to visit you, the secrets of your heart as to God Himself, together with all the sisters, and receiving spiritual instruction from him in everything, even the smallest thing.

When you had remained in such obedience in this monastery for three years, your father and instructor came to love you according to God; and likewise all the sisters came to love you, and your spiritual father wished to entrust to you, out of holy obedience, the care for the holy sisters. You did not in the least seek this or wish it; but knowing the power of holy and Divine obedience, and that obedience is life while disobedience is death, even against your will you bent your neck under the good yoke of Christ's obedience, and took upon yourself Christ's light burden (cf. Matt. 11:29, 30) of caring for the salvation of the holy sisters who had been gathered in the name of Christ and who gave themselves voluntarily over to you in holy obedience. Taking up this heavy weight, you had a certain hope that not you, but your spiritual father would guide both you and all the sisters, and that all the weight of guiding the souls of the holy community would lie on him and not on you. And therefore you did pass through holy obedience with unutterable joy, submitting in everything to the holy Father as to God Himself.

And thus, having lived for two years after becoming Superior, by God's allowance various and many temptations and infirmities of soul came upon you, and your faith and love toward your spiritual father decreased, together with all the other things which you have revealed to me in detail. After you had lived for two years in such a multiform devastation of soul, your spiritual father and teacher departed from temporal into eternal life; and then the eyes of your soul were opened and you began to realize the emptiness of your soul, and of what an instructor in God you had been deprived. And calling to mind the devastation of your soul which had ensued, you wept and lamented, and all but came into despair from the great grief and sorrow of your heart; and you write to me, praying and entreating with many tears, that I might write you something for spiritual consolation.

Not disdaining your entreaty—even though I have no art at all for writing to anyone, and I am unlearned and unskilled—I write to your worthiness and beg and counsel you not to grieve overmuch or despair concerning the former trial and infirmity of your soul, but, with undoubting hope in God's mercy, to place before God a true beginning of true repentance for the past infirmities, and to repent with your whole heart and soul and entreat forgiveness of His goodness. And He, being a God Who is good and loves mankind, rejoicing in your true repentance, as He has forgiven all sinners who have repented, will forgive you also all your transgressions, without any doubt.

It also comes to my mind, O Honorable Lady, that Christ the Savior, our true God, when He wished to entrust the world to His chief disciples and Apostles Peter and Paul, so that they might preach in it His Gospel and by their preaching might instruct those who believed in Him in the true knowledge of God and the keeping of His commandments, and so that they might be merciful to sinners and the more easily forgive the transgressions of those who repent—by His Divine and unattainable decrees allowed that Peter should renounce Him three times and Paul should persecute and devastate His Church. And after Peter's true repentance and Paul's miraculous coming to believe in Christ, both of these Holy Apostles, inasmuch as they had known in themselves the weakness of human nature, were therefore most merciful, in the likeness of Christ the Lord, to those who transgressed and truly repented; and as they bore the burden of everyone on themselves, so also they inspired all to this, saying: *Bear ye one another's burdens, and so fulfill the law of Christ* (Gal. 6:2). Was it not somewhat in this fashion that Christ the Savior, by His unsearchable decrees, allowed the above-mentioned trials and infirmities of soul to come upon you also, so that having beheld the more completely for a long time, as in a mirror, the infirmity of your soul and the weakness of human nature, you might learn to bear the infirmities of the weak and might be more inclined to have mercy on them in the spirit of meekness? Therefore, repenting before God, glorify His unfathomable Providence, which most marvelously ordains the salvation of those who fear Him and repent.

But since, all-honorable Lady, from the reading of Patristic books you did conceive the desire to obtain a true instructor who would instruct you on the path of salvation, and having found such a one with God's help, you did remain with him in true obedience and did keep the holy sisters also in such obedience, and you have also known in very deed and experience the fruits of blessed obedience and the fruits of cursed disobedience—therefore, there is need to write to your worthiness only a little regarding holy obedience.

Divine obedience is something so necessary for the true pleasing of God, that without it it is not at all possible to please God. Therefore, all-holy obedience was planted by God in three places: in the heavens, in paradise, and on earth. In the heavens, among the heavenly powers; in paradise, in the first-created men; and on earth, in the holy disciples and apostles of the Lord. In all three of these places there appeared the fruit of most blessed obedience and also the fruit of thrice-cursed disobedience. In the heavens, all the heavenly powers, remaining by their good will in obedience to God, were vouchsafed, being enlightened by the Holy Spirit, to remain eternally in Him. But the devil, being from the Angelic order, by his own free will fell away from obedience, and becoming proud, was cast down from the heavens together with all the fallen-away powers of the same Angelic order who freely obeyed his impious counsel; being deprived of the Divine light, they became darkness by their own will, and were made eternally enemies of God and of the salvation of right-believing Christians. Behold how the fruit both of obedience and of disobedience was manifested in the heavens.

In paradise, as long as the first-created ones remained in true obedience to God, they took sweet enjoyment in beholding God face to face and in multiform gifts of the Holy Spirit. But when of their own free will, obeying the counsel of the devil and falling away from obedience, they became proud, desiring to be equal to God, then they received the sentence of death from God and were banished from paradise, and were the cause of death for the whole human race. And if the Son of God by His obedience unto death to God the Father had not destroyed the disobedience of Adam, there would have remained for the human race no hope at all for salvation from death and eternal perdition. Behold how in paradise, in the first-created ones, the fruit of obedience and of disobedience was shown.

On earth, Christ the Son of God, having come down from Heaven not to do His own will but the will of the Father Who sent Him, to Whom He was obedient unto death, the death of the Cross, planted His Divine obedience in His holy disciples and Apostles. Remaining in it even unto death, they were enabled by their preaching to bring the world to the knowledge of God, and now with Christ their Lord and Teacher they reign in the heavens. But the thrice-cursed Judas, who fell away from obedience and in place of the Lord obeyed in all things the devil, fell into despair, hanged himself, and perished eternally with soul and body. Behold how on earth the fruit of obedience and of disobedience was manifested.

This Divine obedience, planted by Christ God Himself in His holy disciples, passed over to the holy Angelic monastic order, in which many shone forth like the sun in holy obedience and pleased God perfectly. And, indeed, the whole monastic order is founded upon holy obedience; and in ancient times, whether in common life, or in the royal way (that is, where two or three are together), or in the deserts, for the greater part they began their life with obedience, and thus by God's grace they escaped demonic deceptions. But for those who have begun the monastic life in a self-willed manner there have often followed many demonic deceptions, from which may the Lord deliver us by His grace.

Divine obedience, therefore, is greatly to be praised, as it is, according to the teaching of St. John of the Ladder and other Holy Fathers, the mother of the foundation of all the Gospel commandments, namely, love, which is made perfect by obedience, as the Lord has said: *If ye love Me, ye will keep My commandments.* And again: *He that hath My commandments, and keepeth them, he it is that loveth Me.* And again: *He that loveth Me not keepeth not My words* (John 14:15, 21, 24). And the keeping of God's commandments and His words is nothing else than perfect obedience toward Christ the Lord. Divine obedience is such a great virtue before God that, according to the common teaching of many Saints, true doers of obedience, who have remained to the end of their life in true obedience, receive a martyr's crown from Christ the Lord. For the cutting off of their own will and understanding in everything before the superior is reckoned by Christ, in the day of His righteous rewarding according to deeds, as a mental and voluntary shedding of blood for His name.

Therefore, O Honorable Lady, keep the community of the holy sisters in such a Divine and holy and thrice-blessed obedience, not otherwise than according to the true understanding of the Divine Scriptures as it is handed down and taught by our holy and God-bearing Fathers. Instruct them on the path of salvation, presenting yourself to them, being strengthened by God's help, as an example of every good work—with a diligent fulfillment of the commandments of the Gospel, with love for God and neighbor, with meekness and humility, always with the most profound peace of Christ toward all, with a motherly mercifulness toward them, with patience and longsuffering, with tearful entreaty and consolation, inspiring them to every good work, bearing with the love of God all their burdens and infirmities, burning with love of God for them as for sisters and disciples of Christ, diligently instructing them in true obedience to God in all things and in the cutting off, and even more, the mortification of their opposing will and of the working of their mind and understanding.

But consider yourself, in the secret place of your heart and soul, as dust and ashes before God (cf. Gen. 18:27), as evil and sinful above all others. Force yourself to offer yourself as an example to the holy sisters also in the keeping of the commandments of the Holy Fathers and in bodily labors according to your strength, if you are able, in standing at the rule of prayer in church, in prostrations and bows. Further, perform the cell rule established by the Holy Fathers in the fear of God, with prayers and psalmody and reading. Likewise, read diligently and with great heedfulness and testing the Patristic books on prayer performed by the mind alone in the heart, which is the truest and most God-pleasing monastic labor; and if with God's assistance you understand the true meaning of it from the teaching of the Holy Fathers, then force yourself also to do it, calling on God for help, and you will obtain from it great profit for your soul. Force yourself to judge no one; for there is only one righteous Judge, Christ the Lord, who will give to each according to his works; but only judge yourself and you will not be judged at His terrible second coming. Forgive with your whole heart the transgressions of any who have sinned against you, so that your Heavenly Father may forgive you your transgressions (cf. Matt. 6:14). And what more shall I say? Constantly force yourself with your whole soul to fulfill all the commandments of the Gospel, having all your hope for the salvation of your soul in God's mercy alone, without any doubting. For your previous infirmities and transgressions of soul, which have occurred by God's allowance, may God forgive you by His grace and love for mankind, and may He bless you, both in this age and in the age to come.

As for writing to me: write with all boldness, and for the Lord's sake I entreat you, write to me, unworthy as I am, in detail about your common life, and the church and refectory rule, and your food, and the whole ordering of your life. May the Lord Jesus Christ our true God, who said, *Where two or three are gathered together in My name, there am I in the midst of them* (Matt. 18:20), by the prayers of His Most Holy Mother, our Lady the Theotokos and Ever-Virgin Mary, and of all the Saints, be in the midst of you who have gathered in His Most Holy Name, unto the ages. Amen.

The unworthy entreater of God and all-fervent wisher of the complete flourishing in the Gospel commandments of Your Honorableness with all the holy sisters gathered in the name of Christ,

Archimandrite Paisius
of the Holy Neamts Monastery of the Ascension
and the Secu Monastery of the Forerunner, Moldavia.

Some time after receiving this letter, Righteous Martha decided to go to Moldavia and to be under St. Paisius' guidance, but she received from God a mystical indication of her imminent death, and so did not go.

CHAPTER THREE

A Letter of Elder Sophronius

ABBOT OF NEAMTS MONASTERY AND SUCCESSOR
OF ST. PAISIUS VELICHKOVSKY

A T YOUR REQUEST, which reached us after the repose of our Blessed Elder Paisius, we sent you, with the blessing of Christ's love, a reply accompanying our letter of thanks of last year, which although not very verbose, but in the simplest terms, might perhaps be a solution to your Christ-loving thoughts and desires. Fr. Athanasius, a monk who often resides in the village of Palekh with the iconographer Athanasius Nikitich, in his letter written back on August 16th, 1795 (which reached us this year [1796] on April 26th) stated that you had asked him to write to us about various books, to be sought out here and sent to us to be copied; and likewise to send two drawings of the Wonderworking Icon [of Neamts] and a portrait of our reposed Elder Paisius of blessed memory. Unfortunately, the letter of Fr. Athanasius was detained somewhere for a long time. Nonetheless, those books are already being copied, and after they have been copied, we will truly send them to you with the drawings of the Wonderworking Icon and a portrait of our Blessed Elder, at a reliable opportunity. Rest assured that we are happy to be of service to you, as to a great benefactress. We have still only received three of the books of *The Philokalia* at the monastery but we hope that Athanasius Nikitich, out of his warm regard for us, will not stop trying to send the rest, for which we are most obediently thankful to you and to your entire community gathered by God.

What God will dispose to do about the other half of *The Philokalia,* we also wish to know. According to the latest news, it seems fitting to expect the assurance of both the printing of such books in our God-sustained Russian Fatherland as well as every kind of goodness, as there is rumor here of unhindered freedom there. May the Heavenly Father bless and glorify and may He confirm the supreme Russian authority, and authorities from every land, for their good disposition, to the glory of His All-holy Name, in all things according to their heart. May He shield their kingdom with the full armor of His righteousness, steadfastly, striking with terror all visible and invisible enemies, to the consolation of rest and righteousness and true piety, to the rejoicing of Godly souls, who submit in a holy manner to His all-holy will! May all the delights and the blessing of God's compassions and His condescension rest upon you always and may He accomplish all your desires. Most sincerely desiring this for you, O Honorable Lady, and all your beloved sisters in Christ, we are grateful forever with special Godly reverence for you in Christ's love. O Honorable Lady with all your God-beloved sisters in Christ, our most merciful benefactor, we are your lowliest servants and most sincere intercessors for ever.

Elder Sophronius,
Archimandrite of the Holy Ascension Neamts
and Holy Forerunner Secu Monasteries
with the brethren

August 12, 1797
Moldavia-Wallachia
Holy Ascension Neamts Monastery

CHAPTER FOUR

A Letter of Fr. Athanasius

MONK OF THE HOLY MOUNTAIN
AND DISCIPLE OF ST. PAISIUS*

To the Superior of the Arzamas Womens' Coenobitic Monastery, Mother Maria Petrovna and the God-gathered Brides of Christ:

REJOICE IN THE LORD!

Although I do not know your holiness personally, however, you were not entirely unknown to me when I was laboring in Moscow at the Novgorod Archbishop's *Metochion* for the printing of the first book of *The Philokalia* or *Dobrotolyubie.* Furthermore you should recall that many of the translations printed in the book *The Philokalia,* I had previously brought from the reposed Elder Paisius to Russia: not for my own idle self-interest and appetite, but for my salvation, for the common benefit of the monks. Having finished the translation of the other book of *The Philokalia* five years ago, and on account of my insatiable desire for the Patristic books, I returned again to Elder Paisius. Since his blessed repose up until now, I was on Mount Athos. I arrived here at Neamts from Mount Athos eight days ago to see the present Elder and my spiritual father, Archimandrite Sophronius.

At the same time I learned from his holy lips that the newly translated and recopied book of St. Barsanuphius** which he intended to send to you is now absolutely ready. No matter how tired I was from my journey by

---

* *The Life and Writings of the Elder of Moldavia, Paisius Velichkovsky,* third ed. (Moscow: Kozelsk Optina Monastery of the Entrance, 1892) pp. 253-255.

**This manuscript was later published by Optina Monastery: Barsanuphius and John, Sts., *Guidance Toward Spiritual Life* (Moscow: Kozelsk Optina Monastery of the Entrance of the Theotokos, 1855).

The main church of the Ascension of the Lord at Neamts Monastery in Moldavia, where Fr. Athanasius lived. St. Paisius Velichkovsky was buried under this church.

land and sea, I marveled exceedingly at the Elder's love toward you, in that while he had not yet succeeded in making a copy for the nourishment and reading of his own brothers, he wanted to send the last copy to you. Likewise, I rejoiced at your great zeal and the ardor which you have for such a priceless treasure, that is, for the book of St. Barsanuphius, to learn of it at such a distance and to untiringly strive to obtain it for your community. I make known to you, to the spiritual mothers and sisters, how greatly I, the wretched one, have labored in Neamts so that I might read it even once or twice. The Elder blessed me not only to read it but to copy it out, but because of my age and weakness I could not copy it out. It is very long; anyhow I read it through, and with a blessing I began to read the draft copy. He ordered the copy in final form, for the purpose of mailing to you, to be bound and sent together with the icon to Iasi. Learning of this, several of the brethren began to humbly entreat the Elder that he first satiate his immediate children. The Elder was rent with sorrow on two sides, for you and for his own disciples, for not only some of the brethren, but none of the spiritual fathers had read this book. The Lord, compassionate and merciful, O most beloved mother and sisters, has not despised your entreaty: the Elder learned from an apprentice copyist that another book of St. Barsanuphius was already half-copied in final form in good quality calligraphy. Several brothers decided, for the sake of speed, to finish it off in a cursive rather than semi-uncial script. But purely-printed and well-copied books encourage greater reading and delight the reader, while books copied in cursive entirely discourage one from reading. Hence the Elder enjoined one copyist to finish the book, and another following behind him to read and correct the mistakes, and decided not to send these brothers in the meantime to any other obedience.

So be patient a little while and be hopeful that soon you will receive what you desire, and you will have ineffable joy. I will help to speed things in this matter as much as I can. For in the Neamts Monastery alone three books are needed: one for the library, another for reading in church and in the refectory, and a third for the brothers to read in their cells. Likewise, one is needed in Secu. However, in light of all this I assure you that your desire will be satisfied first of all. I, in your stead, am exerting all my effort and care here in every way possible to finish them soon and to send them to Moscow.

Your benefaction is expressly felt. In addition, I request your holy prayers and blessing.

The obedient servant of your Reverence, Athanasius,
the unworthy monk of the Holy Mountain and Muscovite
July 3, 1799
Neamts Monastery

CHAPTER FIVE

Another Letter of Elder Sophronius

Most honorable Lady Maria Petrovna with all the Christ-loving sisters,
our most-merciful benefactors!

May the peace of Christ the Lord bless your love, unite your community in Godly fashion and grant tranquility to your souls with the hope of partaking of peace in the heavenly habitations!

We were again deemed worthy to receive, on the 27th of August of last year, your reverent letter sent from Moscow on the 9th of March of last year from the Nun Anna by your God-blessed authorization and with the concord of your God-beloved community. We received it with great joy seeing your great charitable efforts for our humble monastery and such truly God-loving remembrance for us by your Christ-loving community. Along with the letter we received the roll of 309 roubles that were sent, for which, likewise, we add our lowliest letter of gratitude together with this letter to Athanasius Ivanovich, which we most humbly ask you to forward to him. Our monastery has been brought great joy that the pictures of the most holy Wonderworking Icon of the Mother of God that is in our monastery which we sent have now been received in your holy monastery with true reverence and we most sincerely wish with our unceasing, yet unworthy, but fervent prayer for the ineffable kindness of the Mother of God, that, according to your devout faith and love for the Mother of God, Her greatly assisting compassion would be with all your requests and hopes, watching over you eternally. Lady Anna writes asking whether or not there exists a special service in honor of the Neamts Wonderworking Icon. Such a service does not exist, but the Paraclesis is always sung, and on Saturdays there is always an Akathist with the Akathist canon as well.

With our lowliest letter, fulfilling our promise given to you, O Honorable Lady, and to your God-beloved community, we are sending you the book of St. Barsanuphius for the consolation of your good souls which have been entrusted to Christ the Lord alone. There is no need to praise us for this, since, as you will see, it will clearly teach anyone who will intelligibly listen to all the virtues, for which the All-good Comforter will bless with gifts of light for the acquisition of the riches of heavenly glory, where Christ the Most-compassionate Giver of gifts will prepare an inheritance for you, and for all the sisters entrusted to you by Christ, as sheep with their shepherd, as children alongside their dear mother. But we advise you in the love of Christ, do not keep this most precious treasury, the book of St. Barsanuphius, under a bushel, permanently in your holy monastery alone, but with zeal allow it leave, for the benefit of others, to those who would care with all their soul for such food. The means for this seem very possible, as His Eminence Metropolitan Gabriel and His Eminence Metropolitan Platon are never too far from you and are fervent assistants in Godly undertakings, and the Very Reverend Fr. Alexander, the Superior, will greatly help your holy monastery. Hence, at your request this book can immediately be allowed publication, for which a prayer of thanksgiving to God will be offered up for you by many Godly souls who willingly kiss without ceasing, with their whole heart, Christ's will alone. For this cause a blessed recompense would be given a hundredfold to your God-loving soul and for all your divinely beautiful community.

Because of your great benefactions toward our lowly assembly, O Honorable Lady, it is our concern, as an expression of our unworthy zeal, to send along with this letter a small book from the writings of St. Symeon the New Theologian, the labor of translation of our reposed father of blessed memory, the Elder Paisius, consisting of twelve homilies deliberately selected like flowers: the first, on renunciation of the world; the second, on the spiritual activity of the Holy Fathers of ancient times; the third, on faith and love; the fourth, on how one should avoid corrupt conversations and judgment; the fifth, on the Beatitudes and the seal of Christ; the sixth, on repentance; the seventh, on repentance and on the banishment of Adam; the eighth, on the cutting off of one's will and complete entrusting of oneself to one's spiritual father; the ninth, on unceasing testing of oneself by the superior; the tenth, on communion of the Holy Spirit; the eleventh, on repentance and the beginning of the monastic life; the twelfth, on how the soul is cleansed through faith and the keeping of the commandments. But the homilies are not designated by such numbers in this small book; instead, in the beginning of the booklet a notice has been added. In addition, please observe how, from the twelfth to the fifteenth pages, the reposed Elder placed two versions in one homily with a line drawn across the page, deliberately showing on top the homily translated word for word from Greek, while below the line, the version from the Bulgarian text, that is, translated from Slavonic; but in each version there is equal profit for the soul.

Furthermore, we are sending with this for your God-loving soul, the translation by our reposed Elder of four homilies, especially for nuns, also compiled by a God-inspired Father, which are composed with refined talent.* With this a pamphlet has been added containing a soul-profiting commentary on the words: "Lord, have mercy."

Seeing your greatly fervent word, O Honorable Lady, as Lady Anna expressed, that you have hereafter promised to our lowly monastery, to the glory of Christ God and His most blameless Mother, to be of service in one thing and to intercede with benefactors in another, and, relying not solely on your Christ-loving fervor, we are emboldened to declare our need to you that we do not have silver vessels for the blessing of loaves [at Great Vespers]; and, additionally, our vestry is very poor in priestly liturgical vestments; and furthermore, in a small skete near the monastery a new modest-sized church in honor of the Entrance of the Most Pure Virgin Mary into the Temple of the Lord has been built, and again, it has need of iconographic work in silver and gold on the new iconostasis. Therefore, we most humbly entreat you to intercede before Christ-loving benefactors that they might donate these things to our poor monastery, to the eternal commemoration of them all as our benefactors, as lovers of the majesty of the house of God, and as ones who condescend to our lowliness, who will be written through the good will of Christ the Son of God in the book of heaven, before the Throne of His Divine Majesty, where the sound of those

---

*Nicephorus (Theotokis), Hieromonk [later Archbishop of Astrakhan], *Four Catechetical Homilies to a Nun on the Day of Her Tonsure into the Angelic Habit* (Moscow: Kozelsk Optina Monastery of the Entrance, 1848).

who keep festival is unceasing, and the delight is unspeakable of those who behold the ineffable beauty of the Lord's face.

Our most fervent prayer is ever-offered to God's compassion for the health of you who do such great things for our unworthiness, in our monasteries and in the sketes which belong to our monastery, in the churches, in every offering. May Christ the Lord bless you with continual perfect health and with many years for the greater multiplication of your good talent of alms and the fervent guidance of the sisters entrusted to you by God's Providence. We are making remembrance for two of your nuns, for the health of Martha and Anthisa. May the Most-merciful Lord grant them perfect health. We pray for the repose of the former leader of your holy monastery, Hieromonk Theodore of blessed memory. There will always be supplication offered for ever in our monastery to the All-merciful Giver of all good things, Christ God, for your God-beloved community, even though we be so unworthy—yet on account of our most sincere desire, may His all-merciful grace dwell in your hearts for ever. May His Divine love be a helper to you, in all the feelings of your soul, that you may behold with the eyes of your heart Christ alone, that you may unceasingly in heart and in mind walk in the steps of His beauty alone, meditating in advance on the heavenly fellowship of the five wise virgins; in all this may His most gracious, undefiled Mother be an Instructress to you, may she establish your mind, that from pure thoughts and a warm heart you will console yourself by the unceasing invocation of the Name of her Son and God, and her most pure name; may your souls be signed with the Divine radiance, transforming, enlivening and making them God-like, that you may love Christ God alone, to the betrothal of the future heavenly radiance: by which may Christ God bless you and all the Christ-beloved sisters in submission to you and the sisters of your holy monastery unto generations, prospering all of you along the loftiest path, in loving peace pleasing to God, extending the years of your life in health. May He bless your holy monastery and watch over it eternally in flourishing stillness in His All-saving Name.

Humbly greeting you and your sisters gathered in Christ with the beginning of the New Year, we wish with all our soul that the All-merciful benefactor Christ bless you throughout the course of the year to spend it in all good deeds of the soul, granting all this to you through the all-powerful prayers of His Most Pure Mother. With these our most fervent wishes for you, bowing to the ground with grateful hearts for your many acts of kindness toward us, and in hope in advance of your Christ-loving aid, we remain for ever with the most genuine respect for your name and for your entire God-pleasing community.

Your all-lowliest servants and most fervent supplicants forever.

From the Holy Ascension Neamts and Holy Forerunner Secu Monasteries

Sophronius the Elder with the Brethren
January 11, 1800
Moldavia-Wallalchia
Holy Ascension Neamts Monastery

V

The Rule of the Sanaxar Monastery

The main Sanaxar Church as seen when the pilgrim enters
through the holy gates of the monastery.

CHURCH ORDER
AND MONASTERY RULE

This Rule, authored by Fr. Theodore, was adhered to in Sanaxar until the 1917 Revolution and the destruction of the monastery. It was published by Tikhon, Abbot of the Sanaxar Monastery, in An Historical Description of the Temnikov Sanaxar Monastery *(Temnikov: Sanaxar Monastery, 1885).*

PART ONE

The Order of Church Services

THE HOLY and Divine Service in the Sanaxar Monastery was celebrated according to the general ecclesiastical order of the Studite rule, in its entirety, without any omissions, as was also done in the Sarov and Vysha coenobitic Monasteries. In particular there were only small differences between the orders of these monasteries regarding the monastic rule of prayer.

The founder, Fr. Theodore, had instituted that in the holy church the Divine Service and reading was to be performed without haste, clearly and reverently.*

The order of the daily church services was as follows:

1. VESPERS

On weekdays Vespers begins at four in the afternoon, lasting one hour. After the end of Vespers a Litia for the reposed is served in the middle of the church: the celebrant and chanters process to the center and sing the stichera

---

* St. Paisius Velichkovsky, Fr. Theodore's contemporary, also instituted such chanting in his monasteries in Moldavia.

of the temple and then the Litia begins with *Holy God,… Our Father,…* then *With the souls of the righteous that have finished their course,…* together with the rest. At the litany the celebrating hieromonk reads the synodicon* aloud, and the brethren also read from the small synodica. Everyone, beginning with the Superior unto the last brother, makes commemoration in church, reading to themselves the names of the benefactors of the monastery.

2. COMPLINE

After the end of the Litia Compline begins, at which, following the Symbol of Faith, the monastic prayer rule is conducted: the Canons to Sweetest Jesus, to the Mother of God from the *Theotokarion,*** and to the holy guardian angel. The irmoi are read and before each verse of the Canon the brethren in the choir chant alternately: *Sweetest Jesus, save us sinners; Most Holy Lady Theotokos, save us sinners; our holy Guardian Angel, pray to God for us sinners.* After the sixth ode the celebrant reads the Akathist to the Mother of God and the monks in the choirs sing the refrains: *Rejoice, O Unwedded Bride; Alleluia.…* After the end of all of the Canons the celebrant reads the prayer to the Savior, to the Mother of God and to the holy Guardian Angel. After the singing of *It is truly meet,…* there is a dismissal. Compline with the Canons also lasts an hour.

The brethren go directly from Compline to the evening meal in the refectory.

3. EVENING PRAYER

At seven o'clock, at the ringing of the bell, all the brothers gather together in church for the evening prayer rule. The celebrating hieromonk begins in the middle of the church.

"O God, cleanse me a sinner and have mercy upon me." *Prostration.*

"Having created me, O Lord, have mercy on me." *Prostration.*

"I have sinned without measure, O Lord, forgive me." *Prostration.*

"O God, be merciful to me, a sinner." *Prostration.*

---

* *Synodicon* is a booklet containing lists of the reposed.

** *Theotokarion* is a book which contains canons to the Mother of God for Compline for each day of the week in the eight tones.

"O God, forgive my transgression and my sins." *Prostration.*

"O my Most Holy Lady Theotokos, have mercy and save me and pray for me, a sinner, to the Lord God and help me now in this life and at the departure of my soul and in the future age." *Prostration.*

"O invincible and incomprehensible and Divine power of the Precious and Life-creating Cross of the Lord, forsake not me a sinner who hopeth in Thee." *Prostration.*

"O all ye heavenly hosts: holy angels, archangels, cherubim and seraphim, have mercy on me and pray for me, a sinner, to the Lord God and help me now in this life and at the departure of my soul and in the future age." *Prostration.*

Then they call to their aid in prayer the Guardian Angel, St. John the Forerunner, the three great holy hierarchs: Basil the Great, Gregory the Theologian, and John Chrysostom.

Then: the Hierarch Nicholas and the holy fathers: Sergius [of Radonezh], Anthony and Theodosius with all the wonderworkers of the [Kiev] Caves, and Zosima and Sabbatius, the wonderworkers of Solovki.

"O holy glorious Apostles, Prophets and Martyrs, Hierarchs, Venerable Ones, the Righteous and all Saints, be merciful to me and pray for me, a sinner...."

After this the hieromonk says:

"O Lord, have mercy upon me and forgive me wherein I have sinned in word, deed or thought, throughout my life, for Thy mercy's sake!"

The prayer of St. Macarius: "O God, cleanse me a sinner, for I have never done anything good before Thee...."

The prayer to the Most Holy Theotokos: "O my Most Holy Lady Theotokos, by thy holy and all-powerful intercessions, remove from me, thy humble and wretched servant, despondency, forgetfulness...."

After this he says:

"O God, cleanse me a sinner and have mercy on me." *Prostration.*

"Having created me, O Lord, have mercy on me." *Prostration.*

"I have sinned without measure, O Lord, forgive me." *Prostration.*

"O Lord Jesus Christ, Son of God, bless and sanctify and protect me by the power of thy Life-bearing Cross!" *Prostration.*

Then he begins on the ambo:

Blessed is our God....

The reader: *Amen. Glory to Thee, O God,... O Heavenly King,... Holy God,...* and after *Our Father,...* the troparia: *Have mercy on us, O Lord,... O Lord, have mercy on us, for our trust is in Thee,... Open the door of Thy loving-kindness,... Lord, have mercy,* (40 times). *Thou Who at all times,... O Undefiled, untainted,... And grant unto us, O Master, in the approaching sleep, rest of body and soul....*

After this the General Intercession is read. During this each humble worshipper, turning with his whole heart to the Lord and Savior Jesus Christ, prays, listening to the humble supplication offered for all people. In particular, entreaty is made for the Holy Church Militant upon the earth, for her confirmation, for the spread of peace, for preservation from heresy, hellish evil and the devil's wickedness.

He prays for the most pious Sovereign together with the whole Royal House, and for all in authority, that under their shelter and protection, the sons of the Orthodox Church may lead a quiet and undisturbed life in right faith, piety and honesty.

He prays for the holy leaders of the Holy Church—for his bishop and the pastors and ministers of the Church, who shepherd the rational flock of Christ, that they might be saved, and that through their prayers he might be saved.

He prays for his father and abbot with all the brethren in Christ, his spiritual father and all laborers of the monastery, trusting in their mutual prayers.

He prays that the Lord save and have mercy on his parents, brethren, sisters and all his relatives according to the flesh.

He prays that all may be saved who serve God in the monastic state in virginity and fasting, who live in monasteries, in deserts, in caves, on mountains, in seclusion and in every place, the fathers, brothers and sisters in the Lord, asking for the remission of his sins for the sake of their holy prayers.

He prays for the salvation of the old and the young, the poor, orphans and widows; those in sickness, sorrow, misfortunes and afflictions; those in captivity, in prisons and, above all, for those persecuted for the Orthodox

Faith by the Godless, the apostates and the heretics, that the Lord would strengthen them all in patience and grant them deliverance from misfortunes.

He prays for the salvation of the benefactors, those who have mercy on them and feed them, who would have them to pray for them, that the Lord would recompense them with mercy, granting them in reward eternal blessings.

He prays for the return to the path of salvation of those whom he has led astray; for the salvation of those who hate him and do him harm and evil, that they would not perish.

He prays for the salvation of apostates, heretics and unbelievers, that the Lord would enlighten them with the light of the knowledge of Him and unite them to the Holy Church.

Having remembered all the living, he extends his humble prayer to include those who have fallen asleep: kings, princes, patriarchs, metropolitans, archbishops, bishops, those in sacred orders, those who have served in the monastic life and in the clergy, for the founders of the Holy Monastery, that the Lord would grant them rest in His eternal dwellings with the saints.

We remember the souls of the servants of God who have fallen asleep: parents, relatives and all who in faith and hope of resurrection have fallen asleep, fathers, brothers, sisters and the Orthodox Christians everywhere, asking the Lord to settle them with the saints where the light of God's countenance shines, in the Heavenly Kingdom.

After completing this all-embracing prayer, they read in order the prayer before sleep:

O Eternal God and King of all creation....

O Almighty Word of the Father....

O Lord, Heavenly King....

Then, after reading all the prayers, the celebrating hieromonk offers the dismissal, concluding with the litany: "Let us pray for the most pious Sovereign and Autocrat...."

The Superior goes to the center and, facing the brethren, asks forgiveness of all. The serving hieromonk replies on behalf of the brethren, and the Superior blesses all the brothers, who then disperse to their cells.

4. MATINS

At 2:30 in the morning the sexton and the brother who awakens the brethren come to the Abbot and receive a blessing. The first unlocks the church and the latter goes around to all the cells of the brethren with prayer, arousing them from sleep and inviting them to Matins.

At three o'clock the bells are rung. After the arrival of the Superior and the brethren, the celebrant begins the Midnight Service immediately, after which Matins is celebrated. The entire morning service on simple days lasts two and a half hours. After the first kathisma a reading is appointed: the Commentary on the daily Gospel reading by Blessed Theophylactus, Archbishop of Bulgaria, read in the Russian language, or the daily reading from the Prologue. The reading is begun by the Superior.

After the First Hour and the dismissal, a memorial Litia is offered, as was done at the end of Vespers.

5. DIVINE LITURGY

Following Matins, at the sound of the bell, the early memorial Liturgy begins in a different church. Certain brothers are appointed to be present at this Liturgy as well as those who have to attend to specific obediences and labors around the monastery.

At 8:30, the bell is rung three times, signifying the beginning of the proskomedia for the late Liturgy. The clergy whose turn it is to serve—the hieromonk and hierodeacon—go directly to church and begin to serve the proskomedia.

At about nine o'clock, at the ringing of the bell the Superior and brethren go to church. All the monks enter the altar and read the synodica, commemorating the health and salvation or repose of the brethren and benefactors of the monastery. After the reading of the Third and Sixth Hours, the brethren in the choir go to their places and those appointed, three or four brothers, remain in the altar to continue the reading of the synodica.* At the litany for the reposed

---

*In the Sanaxar Monastery there were many synodica (small booklets) given by

during the Liturgy, the synodica are read aloud by the celebrating hierodeacon and hieromonk while the brethren present commemorate others silently.

At the Liturgy, during the Communion of the clergy, the reading of instructive homilies takes place, which are chosen at the Superior's discretion and read by chanters more suited to this task. Teachings are read from the homilies issued by the Synod or from the writings of the Holy Fathers: Sts. Theodore the Studite, Ephraim the Syrian, Symeon the New Theologian, the holy hierarch Tikhon of Zadonsk (all in the Russian language), and from others.

6. PROCESSION WITH THE PANAGIA

After the dismissal of the late Liturgy, all the brethren together with the Superior, according to rank, two by two, walk from the church directly to the refectory. The hieromonk who served the early Liturgy carries on a diskos—a special round plate properly called a *Panagiarion*—the prosphoron of the Most Holy Theotokos. The Superior walks behind him. The brethren from the choir, after the exclamation "O Most Pure,..." begin to walk, singing Psalm 144: *I will exalt Thee, O my God....* After the completion of the psalm, when all have entered into the refectory, they begin the prayer: *Our Father,... Glory ... both now ... Lord, have mercy* (thrice) *Father, Bless.* The Superior gives the blessing, "O Christ God, bless the food and drink of Thy servants, for Thou art holy, always, now and ever and unto the ages of ages." The celebrating hieromonk separates three pieces from the prosphoron which has been brought, and, dividing it into tiny particles, offers them on a platter to the brethren. The portion offered to the brethren before the eating of the meal is separated in the Name of Christ, but the portion remaining on the *Panagiarion,* in honor of the Mother of God, is placed in a special place until the end of the meal.

The brother whose turn it is to read the Life of the saint commemorated on that day, from the *Lives of the Saints* by St. Demetrius of Rostov, stands on

---

benefactors, primarily from St. Petersburg. These synodica were read by all the brethren at the litanies for the reposed as mentioned above. At the late Liturgy, the reading of the synodica would continue right up to the Cherubic Hymn, until all the synodica had been read.

an elevated reading stand in the middle of the refectory. The brethren observe total silence in the refectory while listening to the reading.

After the end of the meal, the Superior, blessing the monk who has read the Life of the saint, rings the little bell three times. The celebrating hieromonk says: "Through the prayers of our Holy Fathers, O Lord Jesus Christ our God, have mercy on us." The reader replies: "Amen." The hieromonk continues: "Blessed is God who has mercy on us and feeds us from our youth...." The brothers respond: *Glory ... both now.... Lord, have mercy* (three times). *Father, bless.* The celebrating hierodeacon, approaching the hieromonk who holds in his hands the *Panagiarion* with the portion of the prosphoron of the Most Holy Theotokos, taking it with his hands, elevates the piece a little above the *Panagiarion* and says aloud: "Great is the Name." The hieromonk completes this: "Of the Holy Trinity." The hierodeacon, making a cross, says: "O Most Holy Theotokos, come to our aid." The hieromonk exclaims: "By her prayers, O God, have mercy and save us." After this the brethren sing: *It is truly meet....* The hierodeacon holds the *Panagiarion,* the hieromonk divides the prosphoron in honor of the Most Pure One and says: "Unto the many prayers of our Most Pure Lady Theotokos." The hierodeacon presents it to the Abbot, who eats a portion of the prosphoron and, after him, all the brethren. After the prayer with the exclamation by the Superior: "Blessed is God Who hath mercy on us and feedeth us with His bountiful gifts through His grace and love for mankind, always, now and ever and unto the ages of ages. Amen," the brothers disperse to their cells.

The rite of procession after the Liturgy with the prosphoron of the Panagia to the refectory was instituted in Sanaxar Monastery in 1787, during the abbacy of Fr. Benedict.

That year, following the example of other well-ordered monasteries, on Sundays and feast days, it was instituted to sing the All-night Vigil, and on Sundays in the morning before the Liturgy to gather in the Catholicon and serve a Moleben to the Mother of God with the troparion: *Let us, sinful and humble....* Whether or not the entire Canon to the Theotokos was sung is not evident from the Chronicle, but presently only the ninth ode is sung, by everyone together.

7. ALL-NIGHT VIGILS

All-night Vigils, from the Sunday of the Holy Apostle Thomas to the Exaltation of Honorable Cross (Sept. 14th), begin at six in the evening. From the Exaltation of the Cross until Holy Pascha All-night Vigils begin at two in the morning; on the Sunday of Holy Pascha at midnight; on the day of Christ's Nativity, on the New Year and on Theophany, at one hour after midnight. On simple Sundays (without concurring feasts) the Vigil lasts four hours and on special feasts—for example, the Nativity of the Theotokos, the Dormition of the Theotokos, the Exaltation of the Cross, the feast of the Vladimir Icon of the Theotokos, and the Beheading of the Holy Forerunner—the Vigil lasts for more than four hours. The services on feast days are triumphant and are always served in common by many celebrants. At Holy Pascha the Superior serves together with all of the hieromonks and hierodeacons present.

At the All-night Vigils instructive readings always take place—on Sundays after the first kathisma, a commentary on the Sunday Gospel reading, and on great feasts a homily pertaining to the feast. Sometimes, another reading is added after the sixth ode of the Canon.

On Sundays and feast days, prior to the All-night Vigil, Small Vespers is celebrated, beginning in the springtime at three in the afternoon, and in the winter at four.

At Compline on Sundays and feast days in place of the Canon to Sweetest Jesus, the Canon to the Most Holy Trinity is read at the rule. After the sixth ode, the Akathist to Jesus is read. On the eves of all feasts of the Lord, an Akathist to Jesus is likewise read at Compline.

8. THE POLYELEOS

On days when the Polyeleos is chanted, the service is differentiated from simple services by the fact that, after Vespers and Matins on these days, the Litia for the reposed is omitted, and likewise, at the Liturgy the litany for the reposed does not take place. Only at the early Liturgy are the ectenia and Litia for the reposed retained.

9. GREAT LENT

During the holy Forty-Day Fast [of Great Lent] Matins begins at the usual time, at three in the morning. The service of the hours begins on Monday, Tuesday and Thursday at ten in the morning, but on Wednesday and Friday at nine, because of the Liturgy of the Presanctified Gifts. At the Sixth and Ninth Hours there are daily readings, primarily from the writings of St. Ephraim the Syrian.

10. CELL RULE

From the founder, Elder Theodore, the following cell rule was laid down: in his cell each monk in the evening before going to sleep is to recite by the prayer rope 300 Jesus Prayers: *Lord Jesus Christ, Son of God, have mercy on me a sinner.* During these he is to make 150 prostrations in decades, that is, ten prayers are said simply and ten prayers with prostrations. He makes prostrations in accordance with the church rule: on the days when prostrations to the ground or bows to the waist are made, he does likewise in his cell.

However, the cell rule, especially the number of prostrations, is not identical for everyone. In appointing this, the physical strength of each person is taken into consideration, and this depends upon the discretion of the confessor or elder—the spiritual director.

PART TWO

The Rule of the Monastery

One thing is necessary beyond doubt for each monk—that he should persevere in unceasing prayer, according to the commandment of the Apostle: *Pray without ceasing* (I Thes. 5:17). The Apostle commands noetic prayer, that is, that the one praying would always be raising his mind toward God, as if mentally walking before Him, beholding Him before himself. The prayer rope, which is always to be carried by the monk, is a weapon, constantly reminding him of noetic prayer borne in the heart.

Not only the monastic brethren but every new novice in the Sanaxar Monastery goes to every service with his prayer rope for a constant reminder of inner prayer.

BRIEF NOTES

Sanaxar Monastery is governed by the rule of coenobitic monasteries.

All the brethren are obliged to come without sloth to the beginning of every Divine Service. This is the first holy obligation of each one.

No one is to go outside the church before the end of the service.

The monks come to church in their mantles to every service.

From the common supply of the monastery every coenobite is given clothing, both summer and winter, as well as shoes, bedding, light for his cell, fuel and other necessary items.

The refectory meal is prepared daily for all in common, identical for each. Except for the infirm or the sick no one is permitted to eat in his cell: neither the Superior nor the brethren.

The coenobitic brethren do every necessary task themselves and work for the common benefit of the monastery: they prepare food, bake bread, prepare kvas to drink, work in the garden, wash clothing, patrol the forest; at specific times they gather hay or catch fish. Obediences are assigned to the brethren depending on their abilities with the blessing and discretion of the superior.

The treasurer, heading the economic management of the monastery, is obliged to see to the fulfillment of the obediences, and to prepare supplies and foodstuffs for the monastery in due season.

Those who wish to enter the monastery, into the ranks of the brethren, are received for a period of three years for the testing of their character and behavior. Whoever shows himself to be unfit for the monastic life is immediately dismissed from the coenobium and his lay clothing and effects are returned to him.

Chapel (built in 1904) over the graves of St. Theodore and his relative, Admiral Theodore Fyodorovich Ushakov (†1877), by the north wall of the main church. Destroyed by the soviets in the 1920s.
Photo taken in 1916.

VI

Appendices

The graves of Elder Theodore and his relative, Admiral Ushakov.
Photo taken in 1998.

APPENDIX ONE

Uncovering of the Relics of St. Theodore of Sanaxar

During World War II the soviet government took great pains to boost feelings of patriotism among the Russian people. With this purpose a commission came to Sanaxar Monastery during the war to look for the remains of Admiral Theodore Fyodorovich Ushakov, a Russian Naval hero of the nineteenth century. The task was not so simple because the shrine which had once stood over the graves of Elder Theodore and his relative, Admiral Ushakov, had been destroyed in the twenties during the soviet war against belief in God. For this reason the exact location of Admiral Ushakov's grave could not be determined.

Workers proceeded to unearth one tomb made of bricks lying several feet under the ground. They removed two bricks on the west side, reached in and examined the head. It was obviously that of a monk [Elder Theodore] so they reburied the tomb, and looked elsewhere.

In the spring of 1999 a plaque was found in the Saransk Regional Museum. It stated that opposite the wall of the church the body of the Abbot of Sanaxar, Elder Theodore, lay buried. This plaque was borrowed and brought to the monastery. A discolored section of the foundation of the Monastery Catholicon perfectly corresponded to the shape of this plaque.

On April 21, 1999 (o. s.), the monks began their excavation opposite the place on the wall where the plaque was once affixed. They soon uncovered the brick tomb of Elder Theodore. They carefully removed one brick at a time from the top of the grave and uncovered the remains of Elder Theodore. However, during the intervening fifty-six to fifty-eight years since the commission had sought the accompanying grave of his relative Admiral Ushakov, the roots of a tree growing next to the grave had penetrated the tomb at the spot where the bricks had been removed half a century before. They had entwined themselves around every part of the Elder's body. The

Hieromonk Tikhon and others uncovering the burial vault of Elder Theodore.

Burial vault of Elder Theodore.

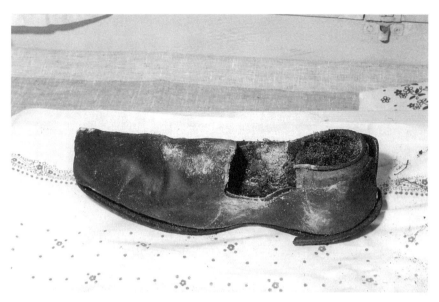

Leather shoe after removal from the coffin of Elder Theodore. April 1999.

The holy relics of St. Theodore.

Reliquary of St. Theodore of Sanaxar, located in
the monastery's lower church.

only parts of his flesh that remained intact were down at his feet. All that remained of the rest of his body after the removal of the tree roots were bones,
together with portions of his mantle, cross and shoes. His skull was found a
little to one side of where it should have been, perhaps due to the handling of
his head by the soviet commission.

Working under a tent, the monks reverently removed the relics and
placed them in a temporary coffin until the date of his glorification on June
28, 1999 (o.s.).

Glorification of St. Theodore of Sanaxar

June 28/July 11, 1999

O N SATURDAY, June 27/July10, we left for Sanaxar, and arrived just as the bells were being rung for the vigil. The Monastery is in a beautiful location in the countryside. Set on a slight hill with a lake near by, the Monastery is surrounded by green fields. It was one of the few monasteries that was not destroyed or desecrated during the Communist period. Though some of the buildings are in need of repair, the overall impression is one of beauty and not the oppressive and heart-wrenching feeling one has when seeing the destruction done to holy places.

We entered through the main entrance gate and into the courtyard outside the catholicon dedicated to the Nativity of the Theotokos. Inside the monastery walls stood the crowds, gathered outside the catholicon, where the services, amplified by speakers hung on the outside of the church, had begun. Though St. Theodore is apparently not that well known, there were approximately a thousand people there. Upon first entering we were tempted to perceive a somewhat carnival atmosphere, because of the cameras, video equipment and indifferent expressions here and there noticeable. But that was only an initial, fleeting impression. As we stood for a while, we saw an attention and reverence that mounted as all began to prepare for the procession.

During Great Vespers, at the beginning of the Litia, a pathway was made clear leading from the church. A cordon composed of trained militia was standing along the procession route to prevent any tragedies from darkening the event. The clergy and monks processed out of the church, after which everyone followed, pressed by the crowd, not really walking but being moved along in a throng, until we passed through the main entrance gate. We processed on to the small Resurrection Church where St. Theodore's relics had lain since they had been exhumed from the grave earlier in the spring.

The clergy then carried the relics in a wooden coffin out of the Resurrection Church. The cordon of militia held back the crowds, and formed a half-circle at the rear of the procession. Walking at the rear, within the cordon, were a group of nuns from the nearby Iveron Convent. Seeing this, a few of the faithful pushed us through the cordon and we continued our way in peace and tranquility. This enabled us later to enter the catholicon for the rest of the Vigil—only clergy and monastics were being allowed to stand inside the church, as it is not very large.

When we reached the catholicon, we first processed around it—stopping and praying at each side in all four directions. After the procession entered the church, the relics were placed in the center of the church.

During Matins, after the Polyeleos there was a reading of the eulogy that had originally been given at St. Theodore's funeral in 1791. Included were his final instructions to his spiritual children. Afterwards, the ukase from the Bishop of Saransk was read, declaring the canonization of Theodore of Sanaxar. Then began the magnification, which all vociferously sang. The Gospel was read, after which all were able to come and venerate his relics. Because of the number of people this process continued until about three in the morning. We hoped we would be able to come back as we were not able to spend even a few moments praying before his relics.

When we first arrived, we had been a little overwhelmed by the number of people, and did not know if we would have the stamina to endure the long service and the press of the crowd. However, we noticed as the services continued that we could not remember a time when it was so easy to stand and pray. The Vigil lasted from five in the evening until eleven at night, but it seemed a very short time—not for lack of fullness, but for a complete lack of fatigue of any sort.

Afterwards the Prior, Fr. Bartholomew, invited us to eat some supper, either in the refectory or at tables set up outside the monastery. The air outside was fresh and the sky was beautiful, arrayed in a colorful sunset, so we decided to eat outside. It was simple fare: bread, millet, pickles, compote and water, but they had enough to feed everyone there. These meals were provided all weekend. In the course of standing in line, we inadvertently astounded a number of people when they learned we were from America. One woman even burst into compunctionate tears at the thought that there are Orthodox nuns in America.

We were very fortunate that night to be given a bed in the guesthouse. The monks had also set up large military tents for people, and many even slept outside under the stars.

The early Liturgy began at 5:00 a.m., in the Resurrection Church. At 4:55, when we were approaching the church, people were trotting in the same direction at a speed just shy of the bounds of propriety. The reason for this rush was the small size of the church into which all hoped to squeeze—a round, columnless structure, more tall than wide. Inside it was completely packed, so we stayed outside in the cool morning air, where the service was nonetheless audible through the open doors and windows. Shimmering golden sunbeams fanned downward through mottled clouds over the open fields. There were so many communicants that Communion was served for nearly an hour, from two chalices.

Later that morning we went to the catholicon in hope of being able to venerate and pray at St. Theodore's relics before the late Liturgy began. Though few were let into the church, our prayer was answered and we were allowed in and were virtually alone there. We poured out our hearts to St. Theodore—may he be for us a helper and intercessor.

As we prepared to leave, our hearts were full. As is everywhere now the case in Russia, there had been quite a mixture of impressions. Here old, Holy Russia mingled strangely but inevitably with post-soviet spiritual survivors: pilgrims and nuns silently carrying icons of Tsar-Martyr Nicholas II upon their breasts, militia, loudspeakers, children, grandmothers, invalids, dignified monks, those crude of speech, and the transcendently gentle. A great ascetic, a nobleman and humble sufferer, now numbered among the ranks of monastic saints in heaven, where may he intercede for us, for this land, and for the entire world.

HOLY FATHER THEODORE, PRAY TO GOD FOR US!

—Nun Seraphima
Nun Cornelia
St. Xenia Skete

Schema-Abbess Martha (Maria Petrovna Protasieva, †April 30, 1813).

A Letter of Schema-Abbess Martha
"On a life devoted to God"

INTRODUCTION

A YOUNG WOMAN, Olga Vasilievna Strigaleva (the future Schema-nun Olympiada), in her early years strove to live a life pleasing to God. Her older sister rivaled her spiritual yearning and they spent entire nights in prayer. However, her sister was afterwards given in marriage. In response, Olga increased her ascetic striving to the point that she once fell gravely ill.

Having recovered from her illness, Olga Vasilievna not only did not change her desire to dedicate herself to God, but suddenly decided to turn for advice to the Superior of the Arzamas Alekseyevsky Women's Community, Schema-Abbess Martha, about whose God-pleasing life she had heard. The letter written by Olga Vasilievna on this occasion has not come down to us. Nevertheless, from the following letter of Schema-Abbess Martha it is evident what an important part she took in Olga Vasilievna's life. The former, in turn, guided by the great Elder Theodore of Sanaxar, had once also spurned both the vanity of the world and her parent's love and likewise vanished secretly from her parent's house.

A Letter of Schema-Abbess Martha in reply to Olga Vasilievna*

I received your letter through which I see that my advice was to your liking, to spend your life in virginity. I rejoiced greatly over this, that the remembrance of God is still within you. For if many were to look carefully at

---

* *Podvizhniki Blagochestiya,* August (Moscow: St Panteleimon's Monastery, 1909), pp. 71-95.

the fleeting nature of this age and to what end we have been created, that is, not for a temporary sojourn here, but for eternal and unending life unto adoption and inheritance of the Heavenly Kingdom, then, of course, not so many would yearn for present, temporal, seeming delights. Actually, my friend, the joys of this age are merely ephemeral and by themselves are of no benefit at all. But if you desire to seek the heavenly, then truly you will find both temporal tranquility of soul and will be liberated from many sorrows.

If you do not desire to be married, your parents will not be able to force you to do so. Thus, my friend, of course I do not advise you to lay these indissoluble fetters on yourself, but to tread the path of God freely. Do not rely on worldly advice, but have ever in remembrance the Heavenly Bridegroom and the saints of God. As they always strove to live in a manner pleasing to God, take them as an example for yourself.

There is a proverb well known to people in the world: *The spirit is indeed willing, but the flesh is weak* (Matt. 26:41). But if you were to ask them: what did these words of Christ the Savior address and to what end were they said, they would not be able to reply. Christ the Savior during His suffering, when he was praying in the garden saw His Apostles weighed down with sleep. In as much as the weak nature of their flesh demanded sleep, He said about them: "The spirit is indeed willing, but the flesh is weak," that is, they were unable to overcome [sleep] with Him and pray. We are in agreement with Christ's words, that our flesh cannot live without sleep, without food or without clothing, and especially in freezing weather without a coat our nature is infirm. But can these people excuse themselves with these words: "due to the weakness of the flesh" from doing good deeds, from despising what is earthly, from loving what is heavenly? Can they say in this life: O Lord, behold the spirit is willing, but the flesh is weak, because of these words we are not able to keep Thy commandments?

When the Lord demanded through His Apostle: *Love not the world, neither the things that are in the world* (I John 2:15), and *Whosoever therefore will be a friend of the world, is the enemy of God* (James 4:4)—the world is to be understood as the worldly passions, that is, the passionate love of wealth, human

Schema-nun Olympiada (Olga Vasilievna Strigaleva).

glory, and a lukewarm and flesh-pleasing life. How then can the Lord require this of us, while He made us weak?

By these their words, that the spirit is willing, but the flesh is weak, the Creator becomes accused. It is horrible even to think this way and by such a cliché to slander the Creator, as if He created us weak to please Himself. Rather, the Lord requires every Christian to follow Him, to deny himself, that is to cut off his own will, and to carry his cross. Lazy souls, those who love the world, and those who are careless about the love of God, always excuse themselves on the basis of the weakness of the flesh, and they will lead you, also, to this end. Do not listen to their counsels, my friend. They themselves do not know what they are explaining. If dissolute counsels had not been given to your sister—as I have heard of her fervor towards God—she would not have been fettered in wedlock and would not have exchanged gold for silver.

The Apostle writes thus about those who are married, what lack of attachment they must have for everything earthly: *Brethren,* he says, *the time is short: it remaineth that both they that have wives be as though they had none; and they that weep, as though they wept not; and they that rejoice, as though they rejoiced not; ... and they that use this world, as not abusing it: for the fashion of this world passeth away. But I would have you without carefulness* (I Cor. 7:29-32).

The Apostle says to us together with you, that is, to those who are unmarried: *He that is unmarried careth for the things that belong to the Lord, how he may please the Lord: but he that is married careth for the things that are of the world, how he may please his wife. There is a difference also between a wife and a virgin. The unmarried woman careth for the things of the Lord, that she may be holy both in body and in spirit: but she that is married careth for the things of the world, how she may please her husband* (I Cor. 7:32-34).

So what is better? The corruptible and sometimes debauched man or Christ most sweet, Who so loved us that He poured out His most pure Blood for our salvation? Is He not able to give to the soul that loves Him Divine aid, if some hindrance for salvation befalls it? Look in the Lives of the Holy Fathers. Which of them used the weakness of the flesh as an excuse? Did they not rather strive for ascetic labors and not to spare the flesh; were they not ever ready for death, and which of them was ever forsaken by God?

Many say, In the world salvation is not excluded. We will not quarrel that one may be saved in the world, but it is not conducive. The Crown Prince Ioasaph [of India] was able to live in the world, to be joined in marriage, to give alms, to do good deeds. But he considered it tobe difficult to live amidst worldly things and to preserve his soul unharmed by the passions, for which reason he withdrew from worldly temptations.

The other God-pleasers pondered the vanity and deceit of this world, and resolved to withdraw from it and abandon everything: parents, friends, relatives, glory, riches and delights, and everything that is in the world; having hated and despised them, they yearned for another life, that is, to undertake the monastic life. Having gathered one by one, they built monasteries and instituted monastic rules. They strove to dispel the evil lusts and faults which lured them into deception in order to uproot the desire of them from their heart and memory, and to instead implant in their hearts the love of God and the desire for Divine joys.

If it were more conducive to be saved in the world, for what reason would they have withdrawn from the world into monasteries? The God-pleasers called the world a sea, and for this sake they did not desire to swim in the sea, fearing to be overwhelmed by the waves of life, and instead headed for a harbor, that is, for life in the monastery, for the sweet salvation of their souls. I advise you, my beloved one, to likewise withdraw from worldly temptation, which brings great harm to the soul. A soul which has seen and heard all manner of sights and sounds, can be greatly harmed by all of them—and especially a soul which endeavors to be wedded to Christ, the Heavenly Bridegroom. The soul must preserve itself from everything so as to keep the heart pure from all passions, and not to be defiled by thoughts, or to apply its love to anything earthly.

In this world it is very difficult for one who absolutely loves God, and it is torture to live in sins.

From your letter I see your longing to come to our monastery. This would be very profitable for you. You could see the God-preserved Sarov and Sanaxar Monasteries and see our father and instructor Hieromonk

Theodore, who leads an absolutely God-pleasing life, and hear instructions for your life. It would not be bad if you tried to spend more time with us. You must hope in God's Providence coupled with your own striving, but the Lord is ready to help. Do not simply hope and leave it at that; but with hope in God's mercy undertake the task. You fear the destruction of the house, but this will not befall you, in as much as Christ clearly said: *Whosoever cometh to me and heareth these sayings of mine and doeth them, I will liken him unto a wise man, which built his house upon a rock* (Matt. 7:24), that is, a house founded upon the commandments of God, and the floods will not be able to shake it. *Everyone that heareth these sayings of mine and doeth them not shall be likened unto a foolish man, which built his house upon the sand* (Matt. 7:26), and the destruction of that house will be great from the flood. Thus, if you do not wish the destruction of your house, do the commandments of God; strive to live in a God pleasing way and have a firm intention to make amends in the work of God, thus will your house be upon a rock.

I advise you, my friend, henceforth to write to us about your thoughts that lead you to despair, which we will try to comprehend. Then our most wise instructor [Elder Theodore], who has received from God because of his manner of life the gift of discernment, will comment upon them, and we in turn will write back to you.

Many interpret the word of God according to their weaknesses and their passions and lead others to despair. For this cause the Apostle writes, *be not wise in your own conceits* (Rom. 12:16), but *comparing spiritual things with spiritual* (I Cor. 2:13). Again he says: *the word of God is a sharp two-edged sword* (cf. Heb. 4:12), with both sides sharp. A person can defeat the enemy with one side, and with the other he can cut off despair; in the same way we also see many who perish from their own discernment and vain reasoning. Many schisms and heresies sprout forth from this: a man receives the word of God and interprets it in his own way and upholds for the truth his reasoning, and begins to harm other innocent ones. Beware, for the sake of God, of falling into diverse reasoning, and especially protect yourself from the enemies of our mother the Holy Church, that is, from schismatics. They quickly put to death the souls of uneducated people; they turn the faithful away from God's Church, from Holy Communion; and they lead them into extreme hopelessness concerning their salvation, as if no longer can anyone be saved at the present time. They expound all kinds of wickedness, as if there were no longer any salvation in God's Church for her true children, and as if the faith has been changed. But they are absolutely wrong: the Church of God has been founded on rock, and the gates of hell shall not prevail against her. Beware, my friend, of listening to their words, as of deadly poison.

You write, my friend, that your intention will be displeasing to your parents, and you tremble on their account that they might learn of this. For this reason I present to you again on this subject the Lives of the Holy Fathers. Take them for an example, how neither their parents' strictness, nor threats, nor tears, nor kindness, nor anything could cause them to waver from their good intention or to turn away from the path of Christ. Seldom does one read the Life of a saint in which his parents let him go in a kind, orderly way, and especially those [parents] invested with temporal wealth and bound to the vanities of their age—such ones always hinder their children [on the path] to salvation. The children's gaze was not directed at this world but they yearned to follow Christ, nor did they set aside their intention, according to the saying: Better to grieve, in a small matter, one's parents according to the flesh, than the Lord Who has created us.

Read about St. Theodosius of the Kiev Caves and about how his mother set herself against him, repeatedly chased after him and, having beaten him, led him home bound. His soul, burning for Christ, did not waver in the least: by his patience he overcame his mother's ferocity. Finally, his mother herself went to a convent. If he, not wishing to grieve her, and even to please her, had lived in the world for several more years, then he too might have wavered in his resolve. It is so dangerous for those who desire to be betrothed to Christ to linger in the world. I can not even describe to you how imperceptibly this spark can be extinguished, which God in His love for mankind has ignited in us. From the world-loving counsels of worldly people one immediately grows weak and immerses oneself in the world, to the extent that one no longer even wants to be reminded about Christ's path. I, a sinner, have experienced all this personally, how an individual in the midst of worldly conversations grows cold and loses his fervor toward God.

I wish both for my own soul and likewise equally for yours that you would serve Christ the Savior in your youth, as we see our holy mothers of noble birth did: Sts. Eupraxia, Apollonaria, Euphrosyne, Xenia the Wanderer, and the other Euphrosyne of Polotsk. They did not delay their intention until they reached their old age, but leaving behind all the attractive things of this world, they ran quickly after Christ, which I desire you also to do, my friend, and I entrust you to God's protection.

I remain the desirer of your salvation,

Maria Protasieva
December 31, 1790.

Postscript

Olga Vasilievna secretly ran away from her parents' house to the Arzamas Alexeyevsky Community and after about two years she received her parents consent to stay there. She became the main assistant of Schema-abbess Martha. Following the latter's repose in 1813, she was elected superior of the same monastic community. She reposed in 1828 as the Schema-nun Olympiada.

BIBLIOGRAPHY

Barnabas (Saphonov), Archimandrite. *Biography and Teachings of the Elder Hieromonk Theodore (Ushakov), Restorer and Abbot of Sanaxar Monastery* (in Russian). Temnikov: Sanaxar Monastery, 1992.

Bolshakoff, Sergius. *Russian Mystics.* Kalamazoo, Michigan: Cistercian Publications, 1976.

Brief Instructions of Elder Theodore, Abbot of the Sanaxar Monastery (in Russian). Moscow, 1847.

Chebotarev, Basil Ivanov. "Memoirs by Chebotarev of the Life of St. Tychon of Zadonsk." In *A Treasury of Russian Spirituality,* edited by G. P. Fedotov. London: Sheed and Ward, 1950.

Clement (Sederholm), Hieromonk. "On Desert-dwelling in the Roslavl Forests" (in Russian). In Juvenal (Polovtsev), Archimandrite. *Optina Elder Moses: Biography and Notes.* Platina, California: St. Herman of Alaska Brotherhood, 1976.

"Elder Hieromonk Theodore." In *Biographies of National Ascetics of Piety of the 18th and 19th Centuries* (in Russian). Volume Two. Moscow: St. Panteleimon's Monastery, 1906.

Gorodetzky, Nadejda. *St. Tikhon Zadonsky, Inspirer of Dostoevsky.* London: SPCK, 1951.

Historical Outline of the American Orthodox Spiritual Mission (Kadiak Mission 1794-1837) (in Russian). St. Petersburg: Valaam Monastery, 1894.

Life of Fr. Theodore, Former Abbot of the Sanaxar Monastery (in Russian). Moscow, 1847.

Life of Our Father among the Saints Tikhon, Bishop of Voronezh, Wonderworker of All Russia (in Russian). 2nd ed. St. Petersburg, 1862.

BIBLIOGRAPHY

Life of Our Holy Father Theodore of Sanaxar: For the Glorification among the Choir of Saints of Our Holy Father Theodore of Sanaxar (in Russian). Sanaxar Monastery, 1999.

Life and Writings of the Moldavian Elder Paisius Velichkovsky (in Russian). 2nd ed. Moscow: Kozelsk Optina Monastery of the Entrance of the Theotokos, 1892.

Muller, Alexander V. *The Spiritual Regulation of Peter the Great.* Seattle: Univ. of Washington Press, 1972.

Peshnosha Patericon (in Russian). Moscow: St. Ignatius of Stavropol Pub., 1998.

Poselyanin, E. *The Russian Church and Russian Ascetics of the 18th Century* (in Russian). St. Petersburg, 1905.

Sarov Coenobitic Monastery and the Notable Monks who Labored in It. 4th ed. Moscow: Sarov Monastery, 1884.

"Spiritual Instructions of Elder Theodore of Sanaxar," in *Elder's Counsels of Certain National Ascetics of Piety of the 18th and 19th Centuries* (in Russian). Moscow: St. Panteleimon's Monastery, 1913.

Subbotin, N. *Archimandrite Theophan, Abbot of the St. Cyril of New Lake Monastery* (in Russian). St. Petersburg, 1862.

Tikhon (Tsiplyakovsky), Abbot. *Historical Description of the Temnikov Sanaxar Monastery* (in Russian). Temnikov: Sanaxar Monastery, 1885.

Tikhon Zadonsky, St. *Works of our Father Among the Saints Tikhon of Zadonsk* (in Russian). St. Petersburg, 1912. Reprinted in London: Gregg International Pub., 1970.

Vera (Verkhovsky), Abbess. *Life and Labors of the Reposed in God Elder Schema-monk Zosima of Blessed Memory* (in Russian). Volume 2. Moscow, 1889. Second ed. reprinted as *Elder Zosima Verkhovsky: Biography and Notes.* Platina, California: St. Herman of Alaska Brotherhood, 1977 (in Russian). English translation published as *Elder Zosima, Hesychast of Siberia.* Platina, California: St. Herman of Alaska Brotherhood, 1977.

Yefimov, Ivan. "From the Memoirs of Ivan Yefimov." In *A Treasury of Russian Spirituality,* edited by G. P. Fedotov. London: Sheed and Ward, 1950.

ARTICLES

"Archbishop Nicephorus (Theotokis) (1731–1800)" (in Russian). *Danilovsky Blagovestnik,* no. 1 (1991), pp. 53–80.

"Letters of Fr. Theodore Ushakov" (in Russian). *Russian Monk,* no. 11, 1913, p. 601ff.

"Notes of Fr. Theophan, Archimandrite of the St. Cyril of New Lake Monastery" (in Russian). *Strannik,* nos. 2–12, 1862. Reprinted in *Counsels of the Elders of Certain National Ascetics of Piety of the 18th and 19th Centuries* (in Russian). Moscow: St. Panteleimon's Monastery, 1913.

Orlovsky. "The Desert-dwellers of the Roslavl Forests" (in Russian). Smolensk, 1904.

Podmoshensky, Gleb. "St. Tikhon of Zadonsk and His Spiritual Legacy." *The Orthodox Word,* no. 3, 1966, pp. 82–89.

"Restorer" (in Russian). *Saransk Diocesan Observer,* Nov. 26, 1991, pp. 2–3.

INDEX

Volume I in the Little Russian Philokalia Series:

St. Seraphim of Sarov

St. Seraphim of Sarov (1756–1833) is one of Russia's best-loved saints, a heavenly man overflowing with Christ-like love, to whom the mysteries of the other world were open. He taught that the main aim of Christian life is to acquire for oneself the Spirit of God. His amazing and supernatural conversation with N. A. Motovilov on "The Acquisition of the Holy Spirit" is included in this volume, as is the "Great Diveyevo Mystery," the Saint's prophecy concerning the last times.

158 pages, paperback, illustrated, $10.00

ISBN 0-938635-30-1

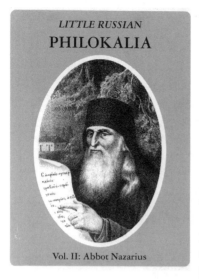

Vol. II in the Little Russian Philokalia Series:

Abbot Nazarius

The Blessed Elder Nazarius (1735–1809) influenced St. Seraphim and was a direct progenitor of the great eighteenth century ascetics of Valaam Monastery. His spirituality reached the New World through the first Orthodox missionaries to America, Valaam monks, among whom was America's first canonized Saint, St. Herman of Alaska.

Here are contained the otherworldly yet practical counsels of our spiritual forefather, showing us the way of repentance, inward purification, and salvation in Christ.

143 pages, paperback, illustrated, $10.00   ISBN 0-938635-31-X

Vol. III in the Little Russian Philokalia Series:

St. Herman

St. Herman of Alaska (†1836), a monk of the ancient Valaam and Sarov Monasteries in Russia, belonged to the eighteenth-century revival of sanctity initiated by the spiritual genius of St. Paisius Velichkovsky. Being in contact with many of St. Paisius' disciples, he was permeated so deeply with the "Paisian Spirit" that he may rightly be considered one of the outstanding bearers of this legacy.

Included in this volume are the original *prima vita* of 1868, a Treasury of His Spirituality and a complete collection of his extant letters.

200 pages, paperback, illustrated, $10.00

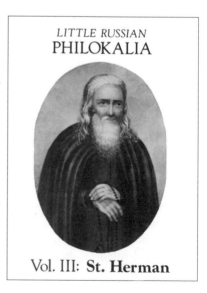
ISBN 0-938635-32-8

Volume IV in the Little Russian Philokalia Series:

St. Paisius Velichkovsky

St. Paisius Velichkovsky (1722–1794) was the Russian-Romanian Elder who rediscovered and made available the ancient texts of what would later be known as *The Philokalia.* On Mount Athos and in Romania St. Paisius was a guide to thousands of monks, introducing them to forgotten teachings on the life of prayer and inward perfection.

Here, for the first time in English, are compiled in one volume St. Paisius' own writings: *The Scroll, Field Flowers,* his Instructions for Tonsure into the Monastic Order, and other spiritual treasures.

151 pages, paperback, illustrated, $10.00

ISBN 0-938635-33-6

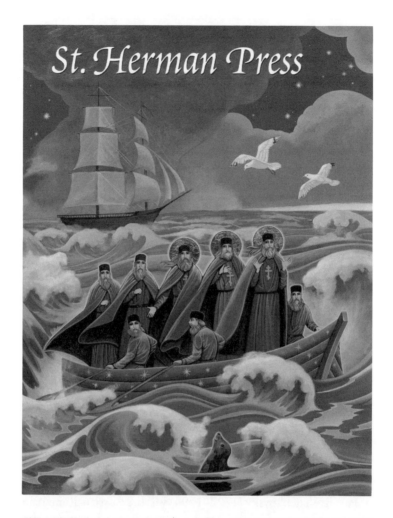

ST. HERMAN OF ALASKA BROTHERHOOD

For 35 years the St. Herman Brotherhood has been publishing works of traditional spirituality.

Write for our free 96-page catalogue, featuring sixty titles of published and forthcoming books and magazines.

St. Herman Press
10 Beegum Gorge Road
P. O. Box 70
Platina, CA 96076